60 for you

NEW MONOLOGUES
FOR AND ABOUT
ACTRESSES AND ACTORS

by Ken Friedman

Cover design by Laura Freeman

*With many thanks to the
heroic staff of
Mumble's Midtown (m.d.)*

And thanks to Phil Giberson and Tsipi Keller.

Author's Note

Keep in mind:

For the sake of reading, most of the monologues in the first section are gender specific. But, with a little ingenuity, can be changed to fit either actress or actor.

Monologues in the second section are specific but can be performed singly or in a group.

And, if a monologue is too long for your audition or class, feel very free to edit it down to suit your needs.

I love New York. I like the smell, the noise, the anonymity of being an actor here and no one cares. I like being in the streets on freezing nights, walking home to save the fare. Beating the bus, avoiding the trains. Chilled. I like the people who are rich. All of them, flashing blond hair; dressed up and dining out and spending more on one meal than I spend for rent; out of cabs, pieces of thighs gliding into sleek white limos; passing me by. In this city, in my career, night seems to come earlier, lasts longer and day is now and things start faster . . . I'm out of it when I'm in it. I have nothing, but I have some of it all. I have wanting. That's what an actor has. Wanting has its own peculiar flavor. Wanting is always in your mouth. I love my hunger.

I'm down in dark streets. On subways that scare me, with vagrants who have resumes: life is flexible and I have a chance. I'm an actor, I have nothing but danger. I hang on, clinging tight to the edge of envy. I am so common that I am glamorous. I have a chance.

You can sit home, if you want. Toasting your tootsies by the hearth. Stay there. But, man, I'm in New York, hungry and dusty, elegant in desire, ugly in desire. And as long as I'm here, and you are there, you have a life, but I have a chance.

It began in January when my friend, Lewis and I, both failed at an open call for an Abraham Lincoln pageant that was hiring two hundred extras. They said we weren't right for a crowd. Not right for a crowd? It was a simultaneous epiphany. Let's make it a contest! For fifty bucks, let's see who could rack up the most rejections for the rest of the year. Now, Lewis is just as rejectable as I am, so I knew I was in for a tough fight. We made rules. We could audition for anything, even the same shows, but, to insure that we did our best, we made a callback count for two more rejections! Let the year go on! I started hot. Four rejections in my first month to his puny one. But, then Lewis pulled ahead with a brilliant February. Turn downs from two Off-Broadway shows; three commercials and a print ad for whooping cough. But, I rallied in March and drew even when I was the only white woman to audition for *Porgy and Bess* to actually get called back. But, Lewis forged ahead with rejections for a Robitussin, two industrials and the Ice Capades. Down by three, I suffered through an auditionless April, but in May, trailing by five I came back big time with a violent rejection from the N.Y. City Opera and two X-rated movies! No callbacks! Lewis countered with No's from a voice-over, the circus and Drama at Sea! Original plays on ferry boats! Then after summer stock, I returned in the fall down by six, but still alive. I was cast in the Off-Broadway premier of *Peter Pan: The Man*! Lewis saw the show and let it count as eight rejections. Then Lewis was Paul Pig in children's theater in Rye Beach; paying his own transportation. Ha! Four rejections. But, I re-took the lead acting for interns at Columbia Presbyterian Hospital as a woman dying of cranial leprosy when I tried to get Blue Cross/Blue Shield to pay for my performance! Rejection. Back and forth we seesawed. In October, Lewis may have entered the Rejection Hall of Fame when he actually auditioned for Harold Prince with his fly open. Not his, Harold's. I countered when I went belly-up at an open-call for the choir at St. Patrick's when I showed up in a mini-skirt. What was I thinking? He had a powerful November with multiple failures in almost every phase of the entertainment world. But, I came off the canvas with a vintage December. I began by being rejected for each of the blind triplets on *As The World Turns*.

"You again? You again? You again?"

Lewis was rejected by a girl he met at a Burger King. I allowed it, because I know how hard he tries. I was rejected as a hand model, a foot model and a dimple model. He was rejected as Santa Claus! I, as an elf. He as a reindeer. It was almost over. December 31st; a dead heat. But, on New Year's Eve I won it all. Yes! Lewis rejected me! The check came in the mail. Wow. All I can say is, to do that, Lewis must have loved me very much.

I'm an actor in New York for only ten months and you want to know how I've achieved the incredible success that I have? Okay. Take notes. At twenty-two, I came to New York. I came from the same place as everyone else. No place. You know where that is. It's where you're from. No place, U.S.A. Because out there it's all the same. Misery, a car, loneliness; sisters. Urgency ... a job. I mean, why? Life's tacky bric-a-brac. Get me off the shelf I'm an actor. So, I came to New York. I took a class and I drove a cab. I almost died. I hit three newsstands.

So, I got another job . . . waiter . . . almost died . . . dropped a tray of hot pea soup . . . on myself. Got another acting job, telemarketing. But, I'm taking my acting class and the teacher is really breaking my balls.

"You stink! You don't grow! What is your motivation? What is your preparation? You have so little awareness." The teacher was an actor, hadn't had a part in twenty years. After four months of his abuse I nearly died. So, what did I do? I quit and I started my own school!

I'm a huge success. Of course. Who would you rather learn from? Someone who's failed for twenty years or someone who's failed for less than one? I'm the most goddamned successful acting teacher in New York. I have a new method. I tell everybody they're great! And you know what? They believe me.

"Very good. Try it some other way. Oh, that's even better."

Hell, I'm not lying. Most of them are good. You know, I love to get paid for not knowing what I'm doing, and this is just the beginning, because as soon as my beard grows in, I'm going to charge even more. And if I start walking with a limp and wearing an ascot, I'll be a millionaire. But, best of all, I'm meeting a lot of girls who think I'm cool. You know, acting is a great career particularly when you never have to act.

I don't know the point of all this, which is probably the point. But, If you want to study with me you'd better hurry, because if I can get away with this, hell, I think I'll become a director.

You want to know how to be an actress? I'll tell you. First of all you watch, while still young, The Academy Awards every year, and realize that that should be you.

Okay, now let's cut to the chase. High school drama, college you're great, etc. etc., so you come to New York (or L.A.) and you are ready, primed for the first major step: The launch pad of your career! You know! Yes! You become . . . a waitress. A waitress and that is when you know you are on your way. Those dishes, those tips, those flirtations, those sticky towels and smelly rags, all part of the first step on the road to Damascus! You are committed, baby! You have taken it on. You're riding the horse! Lance in hand. Banner unfurled, reading in Latin: "Look, folks, I'm struggling!" You take classes, maybe voice, go to gym, tighten your butt, but what does it mean? Nothing. Unless you are what? A waitress! Long hours, short pay and are you alone? No, because you are surrounded by tons and tons of other whats? Waitresses! Who are what? Actresses! Does this get you down? No. Never! Come on, girl, get off the floor and smell the busbox! Wear your sneakers, get neck rubs from the groping staff because you are a— Waitress! Waitress! Waitress! I wouldn't have it any other way, because there is no other way! Do you understand? Then I'll make it clear. Every women on earth who is worth a damn was once a waitress! Wake up. Amelia Earhart? Take Out! Joan of Arc? Brunch! That's right! Brunch. Arc couldn't handle dinner. The Bible? Salome. She toted the head of John The Baptist on what? A tray! And what did her table say?

"Nice head. No fries?"

Waitresses! Waitresses! All of us waitresses. Conjugate: I serve, you save, we slave, they savor. Every actress worth her salt and pepper, in her gut, in her blood, down deep, is a waitress. Nefertiti? Cocktail lounge. Great ass, couldn't add. We are the universal joke; the commonest denominator. We hustle, pool, eat free; not the specials, and read borrowed copies of Samuel French plays; while checking our answering machines again and again and again, during very short breaks at the back tables under smoke; in smells of grease and the crash of dishes. We are a sisterhood. Longing Brides of Stanislavski. Promised to a dream. And is it worth it? Yes. Even if it takes ten years because it was done for one reason. To act. Never be ashamed. Hear me out! You haggard, ragged, foodsore foodwhores; we all will act. Do you hear me back in the kitchen? You immigrant smirkers? When the last salad is tossed, when the final naked potato has been boiled lifeless into a pallid mush: WE ALL WILL ACT! AND, WE'LL GET PAID FOR IT! PAID! PAID! PAID!

Okay. . . . Now, who wants dessert? We have apple tarts, Oreo cheese cake and a really nice pecan pie.

You're supposed to use everything you do. You know, it makes sense. Whomever you meet, talk to, dance with, ride with, shop with and, which also makes sense, use your job. Use. Observe. Find what's unique and interesting and take it, make it work for you. Easy to say. You're in a class being paid forty bucks a week by actresses and actors. That's nice for you, but I work in a deli. I'm a waitress in a deli. The same goddamned uninteresting, yawning, chewing people come in night after night. I've been there for two years. I'm out of new. I'm out of discovery. Where is my growth in this environment? So, I looked in desperation around the store. Am I a customer? Am I a counterman? A dishwasher? A delivery boy? A moody chef who can turn on you faster than a snake? Five days and two nights a week for nothing but money? No. No. No. And then I found it. And I used it. Last week, in class, I became for the first time, I mean, for any actress, a female pastrami. Yes.

"I am pastrami! Smell me! Quivering, hot, tender and bigger than you ever had before. I am pastrami! I am thick and weighted. I wiggle, I jiggle, you sniggle, I higgle! This is a pastrami higgling. What does it mean to higgle? Only a pastrami knows! You fools. Tsa! Tsa! Tsa! Taste me. Baste and waste me. Smell my odors, my secret spices that delight your mouth. Touch fat. Go on. Touch it. Rub my marbled beauty, mister. I am from Rumania. A gypsy that knows you. Hot and greasy I sizzle in your pan. Bite, bite, bite into me. Make me yours. But, I will never be only yours. I am pastrami! I AM MEAT! Do you know what is pastrami spelled backwards? Do you? No? Then I will tell you. Backwards: I'M ART, SAP! Think about it. A pastrami walks. A pastrami dances! Dance, pastrami, dance. A pastrami sings. I sing the song my mother sang. Mooooo. Mooooooo. I know the feel of bread on my back. Ohhh. I know the sting of mustard on my belly. Ahhh. Slide me with unguents. Lather me with desires. Chew my secrets. I will cling to your tongue, slick your throat and explode in your memory. I am arrogance. I am one hot beauty. TSA! Don't turn away! You fat fool. Face me! Pastrami. Pastrami. Pastrami. One night with me and kiddo, you'll never look at Virginia ham again! Tsa! Tsa!"

Well, come on. Admit it. Okay? So, what does the teacher say: "Uh, Yvette, did you really understand the assignment? I don't think you really touched what you were going after."

I can't take him anymore. I really can't! What the hell do you mean, I don't know what I'm going after? I touched everything. What are you? A goddamned vegetarian? Ask them. Ask the class. I was pastrami. What would you have been happy with, Mr. Lester? Quiche? Oh, please. Oh, please. So, I quit the class. I quit it. I quit everything. Adios. Screw them. I like my work. I love my choices and it's the only monologue that I've ever done that made me drool. And, that's more than I can say for Mr. Lester and his class.

I didn't know that Bobby was going to die. I should have and I didn't. He had the disease. It was clear. I saw it on his nose, that purple blotch, but, at that time, I was still too stupid to make the connection. His friends, who knew, made it a joke, because it was meant to be kept a secret. We had been up in Boston doing a revival of a French play and he was very good. He was very funny offstage and very good on it. He was a better actor than I. When we got back from Boston, I used to call him from time to time because I liked him and I wanted to be his friend. As friendly and as close as I can be, which is not that much. And, sometimes, on the phone, he would answer with such terrible despair in his voice. I would say, "Hey, Bobby, is anything wrong?" and he would say no and he would perk up, start doing his routines and was funny. A couple of times we had dinner together. He looked fine. He'd even made his hair blond. And then he disappeared. His friend said he was in North Carolina taking care of his mother. But, he wasn't. He was in a hospital, dying in New York. I'm glad I didn't know he was dying. He was kind then, too.

As an actor I may use that shock, that disbelief and grief. That awful emptiness. I may use it. But, I hope I never do. I hope I have enough dignity to leave it where it belongs.

I'm sick of my resume. I hate it. What the hell does it mean, anyway? This is what I've done? How the hell do you know what I've done? Was I good? Was I bad? Who was I? Who am I? I can be in ninety plays. Do you know what went on there? Do you know what I had to deal with? And a resume is reductive. I don't need a pedigree. I'm an actor, not an antique. Let me audition. Hear and see what I can do. Judge me on that. But, being that I must have a goddamned resume, this is my new one: Last Leading Role: Oscar in *The Odd Couple*. Location: Millman's Motel Theater On The Mountain. Rte. 23, Roanoke, Virginia.

Performance evaluation: sixteen good. Two great. Five that will never be surpassed. . . . Women! A few involvements. None surpassing. Oh, you don't care? Well, I do! I had six weeks near Roanoke! And, you're going to hear about it. Ann was the daughter of the guy who ran the place. She loved me. I was afraid of her. Too young. I'm an actor and this is my resume. The second and third were desperate waitresses from the I-HOP who had boyfriends in the Marines. Both had tattoos. Not the marines, the girls. So much for love. This is my resume. Dead flies in my coffee: twenty-two. This is my resume. Read it and weep. Laundry: three loads! I'm a great actor and this is my resume. Long Distance phone calls made: sixty-seven. Received: two! Where the hell was my girlfriend every night? That's what I want to know! Correspondence sent: twenty-six pieces. Received. One. Thank you, America. I'm a great actor. This is my resume. Sexual fantasies: two thousand three hundred eighty-four! Masturbations: Numbers can't tell the story. Books read: one. Naps taken: forty-one. Money spent: all. Money saved: zip. Reviews: both great but from critics who go to church and probably don't know acting from archery. Loneliness: five hundred seventy-eight hours and twenty-two minutes. Fun: three minutes. Overall rating: six! Okay. Now, how would you like to hear about *Under the Yum-Yum Tree* in Albany? That's my resume. If you want to know me, know me. I'm an actor, do you understand? I am a great actor and that is my proud resume. By the way, I also ride sidesaddle, fence, do origami and process and make my own yogurt. Thank you.

Is an actor important? Yes! Why? Because an actor is a liar. I mean, who, in real life, talks like anybody you've ever heard on a stage delivering a three-page monologue about something that never happened? We lie for a living and everyone knows it, including us, so, therefore, it's fine! Because theater is the lie that does no harm. Is that clear? Out there all the lies and make-believe personalities that we encounter every day as people try to separate us from our money and our emotions, harm us, but, in the theater, these transactions are just! Maybe, that's why it's called legitimate theater? The public wants, lines up and pays for lies, and cheers us when they get taken away by good ones. Because we are the special fantasy that can never be wrong. Mirrors on society? No. We are mirrors to the imagination of society. To the impossibilities of cadenced language, happy endings, sad endings, to a plot that actually finishes in a dead heat with the final curtain. Now, that's worth money. Like Dracula's mirror, we reflect only what isn't there. You know, I love to lie and be someone else, I love to lie and get paid, I love to lie and do no harm, I love to be clever with someone else's words, walk in someone else's clothes. Feel. Feel. Feel for them. I'm getting to it. The playwright confines his myth to paper, then runs. But I am seen; the living liar. I am the outrage in the flesh. I make it happen. I am out there, up and on there, riding on pure guts and gall; technique and talent. Here my heart sings, and here and only here do I give out love: to other actors as we act; and across the lights to the audience. My love goes to them and they love me back. Oh, I can feel it. I can see it during performance when my eyes, adjusting to the darkness, can secretly see theirs, and their smiles, hear them gasp. Here, on this stage, I am a lover. Only here. On a stage, I am a lover. Please understand me. I love . . . with no fear that it's going to count or come back and crack me in the face. And, I'm good at it. And isn't love the most essential lie of all? Was I clear? Anyway, for what it's worth, that's why I'm an actor. And that's why I act.

I was ticked. I mean I went to college to study acting, not to learn anything. Fencing, body movement, and then the killer: Theater History. Who cares? I want to act. I'm in my second year. I still haven't been in a play. So, listen to what I did. A brilliant move. I decided that for this class, I would act the part of a terrific student. Do you understand? What a stretch. Me, the worst student in the world, who became an actor because I hate books and can barely listen to anyone. But, now I had a reason for going to class. I was psyched. Where did I sit? Front row! Thank you. I bought the books. I mean an actor prepares. Right? I read the books. You heard me. I read books! I ANSWERED QUESTIONS! Raising my hand like this. Like this. I TOOK NOTES! Did you hear what I said? And I took them brilliantly. Ben Johnson wrote *Night of The Burning Pestle,* and Sophocles died when he was ninety! Come on, I was good. I got there early, left late, usually staying to discuss a few more salient points. I combed my hair. I combed my hair for ten weeks. That's right. Ten sensational, satisfying weeks. And then came my big moment. The final exam. I got everything wrong! I knew the answers, but I got them wrong on purpose. It was my finest hour. Literally. And when the grades were posted I stood in the hallway pointing proudly to my final D and shared the truth with my startled classmates. I had been acting. Acting. Acting! Wow! Did I open some eyes. Thanks to that the teacher who flunked me, just cast me in *Summer and Smoke* and nobody in the Drama Department will ever take me lightly again. Thank you. Thank you very much.

I had to put an end to it, because it was destroying me. It's the one thing I really don't like about acting; my own envy. So, this is what I decided to do. Wait. First, let me make clear what I'm talking about. Your friend gets a part in a play and you say to her, "Great, oh, I'm so happy for you." Happy for you? I wish you would be eaten by wolves. And, then you start rationalizing your jealousy with these beauties: "Well, she really deserved it, last year her dog died." What the hell does that mean? She doesn't deserve it! I do! And everybody's dog dies! Mine did. When I got my Prune Dip commercial did my phone start ringing? And when I did *Arsenic and Old Lace* two years ago, how many friends did not—never mind. But, I always go. I always go to see them in their crap and I go backstage. I hate telling them how good they are, because sometimes they are! I hate that. But, then I ask myself if I'm a good person. And I have to say: No! No! No! . . . No! It's just not me. So this is what I did. When a friend was in a showcase I sucked in my gut and I went to see it not once, but TWICE! Gagging, I went backstage both times to say: "You are so good, so unbelievably 'there' that next time I'm bringing Mom." Okay? Oh, it hurt! It hurt bad. But I went back five more times! Paid for tickets, brought candy and, yes, I did it. I dragged my mother! And you know what? I started to feel good. Yes! So, then I went even further. I started calling actors just to hear them talk about themselves. And I listened! I did, too! And, believe it or not, I even remembered a few things that they said. They loved it! Oh, the joy in those little voices. Now the fever was spreading. I was soon seeing open calls in the trades and calling friends. "You must go up for this! Not me. You. You." And on my answering machine I left a bright new message: "Hi. Thanks for calling. I want to hear everything. Everything. And I will call you back because I can't live without knowing each tiny detail of your life and if anything good happens, promise that I'll be the first to know, so I can buy champagne!" Well, I started getting phone calls from all over the country. And then inspiration. I began my newsletter *Nothing New*. Which featured very short articles about my failing career and lack of success. Popular? God. I'm selling advertising! Everyone wants to read it. I can't tell what this change has done for me. I feel younger. I am younger. And let me add this for you people listening to this monologue. You are the best and I love you. Why? Because you are all so damn talented, that's why. And if you allow me to come back again, well, may I bring my relatives? I can? Great. Because, THEY'RE HERE! Yes! Waiting outside. May I get them? Goodie. I want so much for them to meet people like you. Mom? Dad? Aunt Rose. Uncle John? Come on in. They're too shy. Wait. Don't move. I'll get them.... Mom ... Dad ... Granny ...

I'm excited, but I'm not excited. I'm excited, but I have a problem. I am finally in a show. Thank you. It's a showcase. I auditioned. I was good. They called me. But, I have a problem. It's a play about the Korean War. Did you ever hear of it? I know. It's just not as theatrical as other wars. But, I'm told, it still has a small but loyal following. Like Bill Haley and the Comets. But, the director says, the Korean War is just a metaphor.

"For what?" I asked. Because, I'm an actor. I must know. "It's a metaphor for the Vietnam War." Oh . . . But, because, there have been so many good plays about Vietnam, who needs another one? But a metaphorical play about the Korean War which takes place entirely in a bunker which is a metaphor for the world, is not only topical, but is also cheap to produce. And as one of my co-stars pointed out, the play itself is a metaphor for writing. In the play, I play a soldier. Which is fine. But, as soon as the curtain rises, I stand and say: "Look! An eagle!"

And I take a bullet to the head and for the rest of the play, I'm dead. No more lines. No activity. I just lie there. It's tough. So, I had a talk with my director about motivation. He said: "You have none. You're dead." So, I say: "Okay. But couldn't I just die slowly? Couldn't I die in someone's arms? Why can't I hang on for a few minutes? Call out some names? How about a death rattle? Listen to this one . . ." No dice. Acting? I could be replaced by a hibernating bear. But, that's not my problem. This is my problem: Do you think I should invite agents? I asked my co-stars, both sergeants, and they said I should invite morticians. I don't know what to do. Will you come to see a performance? Thank you. Because, I am good. "Look! It's an eagle!" You'll see. I am very, very good. You'll come? Great. Now here is another part of my problem. There are no free tickets.

I'm in rehearsals. That's all I want to do. Give me lines. Give me cues. Again. Let's do it again. At night in the bed, in my room, on the street, at the wall, eyes shut, brain insistent. Run those lines. Do it again. At the mirror. It's getting better. I'm finding him, losing me. Do it again. It's the only way. My way. Was I better today? Was it good? I think. I hope. Over again. I was good today. I was. Was I good? Was I different. Am I better? I want more. What time? Where? With you? By ourselves? You and me. Let's meet. Let's run lines. Let's do cues. Let's talk this over. Let's do it again. Let's run lines. Let's do cues. Let's do it over. I want to do it again. I want to know more than the words and the meanings. I want to know so much that I no longer know. In the shower, in my bed, in the street. Do the lines. Know the cues. Run the words. Wear the clothes. Cadences that aren't mine begin to appear in my own speech. Not enough. Am I good? No outsiders at rehearsals. No strangers staring. I'm not ready. I want to see nothing but the stage; hear nothing save myself and my family and be on that stage. Rehearse me and keep the doors shut. GOD DAMN IT! I SAID: NOBODY IN HERE! I want no phone calls. Mail. Or questions. Conversations. Music! Hot weather!

Stay away from me. This is what I have to do. No bills. No laundry. Over again and over again. This and only this and again! I am an actor. This is the world. This is me. This is not me. This is me. I have to act. GET AWAY FROM ME! I have to think. I HAVE TO DO IT! . . .

They came to visit me last week. Mom and Dad. Jesus. Oh, Jesus. Fry me. Shoot me. I love my parents, but from a distance. Please. Don't come to town again. The telephone is bad enough. You know what it is? I can't face me. That's all. Because when I see them I see Yours Truly as they see Yours Truly, which is, quite honestly, something I don't need to see. Actor. Out of work. Damn. But, what can an actor do? They have no idea what this is all about. And I do! And I'm afraid to tell them! They hate what I am. Yes, they do. And I know exactly what they think. We're in the Italian restaurant. I can barely eat the meatballs because I know what's eating them! Say it. But, they won't. "Jason, you're our son; there's nothing we can do about that. But Jase, you are a loser! You are a twat! (My favorite word.) You are immature. A self-deluding, not handsome enough, talented enough, nor clever enough, wacky enough boy to make it. Therefore, we hate you. When you fail, we fail. You embarrass us. You embarrass us in Santa Barbara, in Crandford, in Deluth, in Poughkeepsie. Wherever parents gather; in places where families still exist and everyone knows your life. You are in the Atlas of Assholes. Actor? Oh, you shame us with this little girl's choice. Grow up, sucker! You're never, ever, never going to make it. Pass the pasta. Mmm, is yours good?"

What do I owe these people? What do I owe them? Your parents are there, you're here and it's murder. How can I explain that I am not a fool? How can I explain that it's all worthwhile? How? And, for Chrissakes, what's the use of taking me to dinner when I can't even swallow the fucking tortellini? And after dessert, (spumoni) when we're outside and they're getting into a cab to go to the airport, and they are not rich people, they slipped me an envelope with a hundred dollars; which I took. How could I take their money? What the hell happened to my pride? Where the hell is it? I'm better than this. But, maybe, and I hope I'm not lying, maybe I took the money not just for me and my career. Maybe I took it because of my father's strong hug and for the love and sweet need in my mother's eyes.

I want to be a star. Okay? Everything else is bull. A star. A star. A star. Jesus. That's it. Oh, I want to act. I want to do good work, but everyone wants to do good work. The goddamned baker, the auto mechanic, well, maybe they don't. No, but they do. They want to do good work, but they want to overcharge. Well, so do I. Or do you think I'm going to acting class because I intend to spend the rest of my life eating tuna fish casserole? I want all of it! Shocking? Well, hear this: I want my name everywhere. I want my face on magazine covers, napkins, doilies and towels. I want men. You don't like to hear that, do you? You want me to say: "At the end of my career, I want to be proud of my *oeuvre* and I wish everyone in the world good luck."

No way! I want men who won't even look at me now. Okay, they look. I want sex from everyone I want it from anytime I want it. Why? Because this girl's a star! I'm a star, baby. I want seven homes on six coasts on ten continents. And I want to fire agents. Mucho! Oh, how I want to fire agents. On a whim.

"I don't like your ears."

And, I want scented lawyers to line up for miles to kiss my ass. And, I want to go to reunions, because I have a huge heart and I will be modest.

"Of course, I remember you."

I dream of being gallant to total strangers on street corners; common people who will tell other slobs that they actually saw me, and I was so congenial, so warm. But, at script conferences, look out:

"You call this a scene? I don't. I want it done my way! Do you hear me? My way! Or, I'm walking!"

And if I turn out to be right, I'll take the credit, and if I'm wrong I'll blame everyone else or say that I've learned and grown as an artist. I love that. Artists are always growing. What do other people do? Shrink? Oh, you ones who say: "I just want to act. I want to do good and exciting work." You hypocrites. You snake in the grass, wimps. Go on, play that shadowy game. Con yourself into finishing somewhere in the middle, if you finish at all, if indeed, you're not already through. Not this actress. And the biggest reason why I want to be a star is so that when I have my breakdowns, big, famous breakdowns: "She's in a home again! God, how much longer can that poor woman last? Is it drugs, alcohol or final-stage flab?"

It'll be because I am a star and not because I never was. I think that sums it up. I'm in it to win it. Two, four, six, eight, who is so perfectionate? Me! Me! Me! ... Me and only me!

Have I been hypnotized?

I need to sit down. When I tell you this. Have I aged? I don't want to talk about Kentucky, I don't want to talk about anything until I tell you what has happened to me. It's hard to believe. It's about my folks. No, they're not dead. I could handle that. Look, I'm trembling. I'm falling apart. Hold me! It started innocently enough back home in Elkhart. They went to dinner at a neighbor's whose brother is an account executive at BBDO in Chicago. Thanksgiving. Why wasn't I there? I'm always home! Well, the BBDO guy liked their look. Their look? They look like shit! MY PARENTS LOOK LIKE PARENTS! I'm sorry. I love them. He liked their look. So, he invited them to Chicago for a look-see. A commercial for bathroom fixtures or faucets . . . my parents who have never acted, who hate acting, who think a stage is something I'm going through, got it! They got the commercial. It was shot, and on the air regionally in two weeks. Then it went national. I saw it. Mediocre. It was seen by a casting director in L.A. Contacted! Phone calls! Flown to the coast! It's Fox television. Act? They can barely read. A sitcom. THEY GOT IT! My parents got a sitcom. Hold my hand. Please. I've been acting for six years. I have nothing. They have never acted and in six days, they have a commercial, a sitcom and an agent at I.C.M. There's a son in the show, but I'm wrong for it. WRONG? I'm always wrong for everything! My parents. Why didn't I go home for Thanksgiving? No! I had to go there for the fucking July 4th barbecue and all that greasy sparerib shit! I HATE SPARERIBS! GOD! My parents. Of course, I'm keeping in touch. I'm not a fool. I called them in L.A. last week. Twice . . . They're not returning my calls. My own parents. It's my fault. I should have been nicer to them. Why wasn't I nicer to them when I had the chance? Do you think . . . do you think it's too pushy to send them a photo and resume? Do you? I don't. I think it's the smart thing to do and a little note and, okay, a box of candy. But, that's as far as I'm going. One box, and that's all.

You practice your monologues. I'll invest in after-shave. Why? Because you audition for the role. Who cares? And for the experience. Come on. Or for the important people that you meet and who forget you as soon as you hope for a compliment. Stop jerking around. It's delusional. Listen to me. Okay? You know why I audition? I'll tell you why. For the women! That's right. The trip can be long, the play lacking, the part already cast, but, if I'm lucky, at every open call at least one worthwhile woman who is much better than the script. Am I wrong? It can be an actress, pretty, or the director-lady, sometimes hot, or the cute, young thing at the desk or, and luckily, I have never had to sink this low, the writer-honey; often, not only not overly gorgeous, but frighteningly well-read. Now, the first handshake is so exciting. Isn't it? I do mine like this: . . . Eyes that meet, that click and cling. A smile that is a hook. Ohhh, the first brushing touch of hand to elbow. I LOVE IT! Please, don't think I'm kidding myself. I know what I'm really up to. Is it sex? Sure. But, not only sex. It's about winning.

"Hi . . . nice to meet you . . ."

Touch her fingers, modest smile, but eyes that open up the menu. What an audition I give! Man, I'm good. Hey, it's all acting. Isn't it? Okay, I'll be even more honest. I am kidding myself. I know exactly what's going on. Love-shmuv. I'm just co-opting rejection. I'm a coward. That's all. Changing the game to go after something that I might get, instead of chasing something that I really want. Okay! I'm revealed. So what? I don't give a damn, because this way, even if I leave with no part, no callback, no nothing, I just might leave with a small piece of something; a piece of them. I want that piece for all the little pieces of me, that I've left behind. So, I guess, it's not about winning, it's more about not losing everything. Going in there, standing up and losing everything. That is really bad. Do I care about their feelings? Of course, I do. Am I evil? Is survival evil? How far do I go? As far as it goes. But, so far, not that far. But, at least now, I have a real reason to get ready for those empty rooms and long waits. Now I know what I'm waiting for. And as I said, did I say this? I don't remember, so, I'll say it again: If nothing else, I'm auditioning with a purpose and I smell very good.

It starts in the afternoon. I don't care If I've done the show six times, ten times, even for a month. I start walking. I don't like interruptions. I don't want phone calls. I start walking. If I'm in the apartment, I walk there. I pace and do my lines silently, in my head, over and over and then I'm relaxed. I know it. I sit down and then I walk. With an hour to go, it kicks in again. I get inside myself. I don't want to speak to anyone, but I will. Casual stuff. The other actors are kidding, talking to each other; jokes, complaints, gossip. I don't want to know. Just leave me alone. I'm polite, but not involved. Dinner for me was almost nothing. My appetite is thin. Soup, anything light, nothing to interfere with me and what I have to do. And, then, I do my first few lines again, and the small animal, that twisting cold worm in my bowels, eases. Make-up, costume and at ten minutes I'm already in the wings. I can hear the low drum of the audience beyond the closed curtain. My mouth is parched. My stomach twists. Don't touch me. Don't touch my arm. Between the ropes and the straight edge of black wing flats I see a slice of the stage. It seems lopsided, intimidating. I only want to be good. I want it to be good and I want it to be over. Why am I doing this to myself? My lips are compressed and my hand is rubbing my chest; calming me. Be good. Be good. Be good. You are good. The first speech. I do my first speech. The stage manager is right next to me, but he stares straight ahead, knowing what to do. I hate my fear. Why am I doing this? If I could only remember what it was last night. If I can only remember that after that first step, that first word, I am home in a place more comfortable than my life, in a life more secure than Saturday sleep; in control of every rehearsed, certain word, each step, all angles, all done over and over and over, polished to a certitude.

The curtain is up and I am on. The lights blind me. This is my territory and domain. I am perfect in every step, tone, nuance, shade. I am almost automatic and free as wind within these walls. This is where I belong. Out of the world, in front of strangers, oddly safe. I'm an actor and the stage and nothing else is home.

The director is my brother, my father, my pat on the back; my ears, my eyes, my heart. Tell me what I'm doing. Get me on the road and I'll travel the rest of the way. I'll startle you. I'll find things you never dreamed of. But be there. Be my analyst in the night. My coffee in the morning. Be kind and funny and laugh me through a mood. I have to have you there. Oh, I know what I'm doing. I know how to be sweet; how to get a laugh. I can take the moment and steal the stage. I can open hearts. But, you have to approve. Pull me back, rein me in, give me air. I'll sit through notes and suffer criticism. I want to please. I want to be good. If you treat me with love and high regard, you can have a tantrum every now and then. Remind me of who you are. Block and cajole me. Praise and confront me. Help me find our truth. I am so frightened. I can't tell you how afraid I am. I need to be held. I am an actress hunting a home. I need a mother's hug. A father's kiss. Hold me with your words. Get me through those elevator-shaft days and wide-eyed nights of Hell. Do that and we'll have a bond cleaner than marriage and tighter than blood. But, and this is the truth, and it's nothing I'm proud of: we can go through all this, through all of this and more, but if the critics don't like us, then it all changes. I'll blame you and you'll blame me and we'll all blame the playwright and we'll have so little to say about each other again. It will be as if we barely were. But, if the critics love us, well, then, as I said, our bonds will be cleaner than marriage and tighter than blood. Don't you agree? Excuse me, have I said the wrong thing?

Should an actress have a social life? Hell, yes. I want a boyfriend. I want a lover. And it has to be someone hot. And I know that it must be another actor, a director, or even a writer. Someone who knows what acting is. A man who knows who I am. Know me. School teachers my own age, need not apply. But, older acting teachers or even a college prof.; maybe. That is it. I want a man who knows the business.

I can't take lawyers who are boring, firemen who are handsome, social workers who brood. I want the fight! I want a house full of ego. I love jealousy. To me jealousy, not love, is the key to an honest relationship. I'm jealous of you, you're jealous of me! That's honest. When he acts I want to be pleased, but offstage have constructive comments which kill him. Hey, keep the fun alive. Hell, I've had boyfriends who adored me. TAXI! What fun is that? You want the truth about me? Here it comes. You may not like it. I want my life to be a play. Something wrong? I don't feel guilt. This is no sham. The sham is the sham.

I want my life to be a play. Open-ended and always happening. Today is my audition for tomorrow. And I get better by the day. I want conflict. I want sex. Sometimes it would be better with an audience. I mean the conflict or the sex. What you run from I chase. I am an actress. I want you. I want to live eight lives. I want making-up, fighting, making-up, loving, getting, longing, caring, bleeding, worry, agony, heartache, fire and bliss, but hopefully, most of it will be in public! Everyone I know must know. That's why I have friends. Forget it! You aren't friends. You are my audience. So what? Am I ashamed to use you? No. Because, you love it, and if you don't, you should. Because this girl is on! Don't you dare turn me off! I am an actress in your life. I turn hot to cold, love to waste, find song in silence.

I am bigger than you are; bigger than you want to be. I am reaching for everything and bringing it back to you. Reaching, reaching. DON'T PULL ME AWAY! Am I crazy? You know I'm not. I am the hot, hot, hot girl. Acting and acting now! Do you know about me? But, oh, Jesus Christ, what am I going to do when I'm forty?

It's the relationships that get me. You're you and then you get a job, and the next thing you know, after two weeks of rehearsal, you're doing *Tchin-Tchin* in Pine Hill, Virginia, and all of a sudden everybody in the cast is in love, except you! What the hell is it? And there is one couple who—Tim and Claire—I shouldn't tell you their names, who are so totally wrapped up in each other, it is downright embarrassing. They just met! It's unbelievable. And what about my privacy? Why does everyone have to see them all day long, like, like, well, you know. Damn it. I know it's Pine Hill, and there's nothing to do. Okay! So do it by yourselves. Holding hands and clutching waists. And kissing. Kissing before breakfast. What about me? Look, I've been there. I've had my share. But, always with decorum. Why do actors have to flaunt their romances like they were demonstration models selling tongue, ear and tit kits? I am angry! It's unfair. I mean, where the hell am I supposed to look? They're everywhere.

"Hi, everyone. We're in love! Check out this blocking."

Sniffing, moaning, cooing, rubbing, goddamn irritating! It's happened in every goddamned tour I've been on. Can't actors make love by mail? No. It's always for the goddamned public. God, you've just spent ten hours in bed together, give daylight a chance. And, I'm not overreacting and I'm not jealous. Because, a month after I'm back in New York I run into Timmy at a reading, and he's with his old girlfriend. What? What the hell happened to Claire? Was she hit by a truck? So, I call Penny. Tim's had the same girlfriend for two years and Claire's nearly engaged to a stockbroker. Engaged? How? How? How can you be engaged to a stockbroker and still dry-hump an actor in a booth at the Frostee-Freeze as fellow cast members eat custard and look on? It's wrong and I hate it. Actors. It's wrong. And, I'm never going through this again. The next time I go on the road, I'm taking my wife.

Larry Steele knew the business. You know I've been trying so hard to get an agent, because, what the hell are your chances to make it if you don't have one? But why, if I'm good, am I still looking for, no, hungering for, that one person who can change my life? Why? Because you try to get someone worth a damn to come and see the two billionth devastation of the *Cherry Orchard* in a production that cost two dollars less than his belt. Please. That's why I was amazed while doing *The Velvet Crust*, six performances, don't ask. A stinkeroo so bad that it even made the author puke, when our stage manager said an agent was in the house. I was determined to shine and, afterwards, a card for me. Only me. Everyone else was so jealous. Larry Steele of Steele Talent and Associates. Familiar? It should be. We met for lunch. Thai. And I made every right move. I did not pander, but I did use powerful eye contact, and my smile; this one, was . . . sublime. And so was he. Okay, a little greasy, a touch of oil, but not enough to fry in. He was soft-spoken. He was knowledgeable. And he was very impressed by me. I love that word. Me!

"Let's talk about where you should be in three years. Films." Larry Steele. Under forty; aggressive and wanting more.

"I have a limited roster." He wanted me. "First commercials then breaking out. I have contacts at Paramount." Limited roster? Bernadette Peters! Treat Williams! Austin Pendleton! And me. He said, "To be honest, with some exclusions."

Exclude away, Larry. Exclude your brains out! Do I care? You are my hope, my greasy savior. You are my truth! I didn't sleep that night. I was so excited. I even called home. It was happening. Finally, finally, finally. And oh, God, I have waited for this. Oh, how I've waited.

In just two days I saw him again. On the front page of The *New York Post*. Shot to death by a twenty- year-old call girl who was one of his prostitutes. PROSTITUTES! My Larry! Cold as a carp! As dead as my hopes. Oh, God. Then two cops came to my apartment. Why? Because what was sitting on Larry's desk? MY PHOTO AND RESUME! The cops now think I'm a hooker. Me. I don't even date. "What do you take me for?" I'm screaming. "Are you crazy? I'm not a hooker! I'm not even from New York!"

And the other cop is in my kitchen holding my resume in his policeman's hand, and he's not bad looking, and he says, "Miss, are these the only shows you've done? No television?" Well, then of course, I broke down. I should have said I was a call girl. I should have said I shot the rotten liar! At least then, I would've gotten some press. Oh, hell. What really bothers me is that of the six girls in the cast, he chose me. Was I that good or was I that bad? That's making me crazy. Really. And what do I say to my mother? And it's almost Christmas and I've got to got to get a job. I have to. Are they still hiring at Macy's? Or am I too late even for that?

This happened to to me. This really happened. It was unbelievable. But, I swear it's true. I told you about the play I was in at Billy's Theater Club, upstairs over the driving school? Okay, it's our third performance. The play's a bomb. What can I say? I'm playing the part of a tough guy; the goon who comes in near the end of the play and beats up the miserable gambler in front of his long suffering gorgeous wife. Oh, I'm accompanied by Little Phil, the gangster boss, to whom the gambler owes this huge debt. So, as I pound the miserable gambler, who by the way, is the author, into submission, his gorgeous wife, who is by the way, from Oklahoma and is about six foot two, in order to save her husband, silently offers her body to Little Phil, who really is little. Phil accepts the offer of sex, I stop pounding and the wife, because Phil can barely lift this Amazon, jumps up into his arms and Phil says:

"Baby, let's make the earth move."

Well, now Phil is supposed to carry her off into the bedroom by taking her offstage between the flats and the stage wall. Like this. But, what happens? They get stuck. In full view of the audience. Stuck! She gets wedged in between the flats and the wall. Her head is this way, her feet are that way and she's not budging. The audience is starting to laugh. So, poor Phil, with one huge shove pushes her forward, but what happens is this causes the living room wall to cave in; hanging like sixty degrees and all the stuff; the furniture, the mirror, the drawers come down on the stage with a tremendous roar, followed momentarily by the stage center window and all the door knobs! Clang. Clang! Boom! And dust! Clouds of dust! Well, it's the biggest laugh I have ever heard. And, I'm standing there stage center with the unconscious guy at my feet. What can I do? What? So, I say: "Wow! And, they haven't even gotten to the bedroom." Well, laugh followed by sustained applause. And then some guy in the audience yells out:

"This should have happened in Act One!"

A few moments pass and the lovers have to come back on, but there's no set, just pieces of things, so they literally climb up over what's left of the living room wall and re-enter to a standing ovation! It's theater history! A few more lines and the play is over. It's over. I'm over. The set is really over! And the author's life is over. He's still on the floor, refusing to get up for bows. I feel very bad for him. Well, up until now, we'd been good friends. Now, he hates me. Because I made a

28

joke of it. What could I do? The set fell down. Does that happen every day? Is it my fault? Is it? Why is everything my fault? He's so sensitive. So, please don't tell anybody about this. Okay? Because, I want to. It was great! My greatest moment in the theater!

No, No. I don't mind what you said. You had a few positive comments about my performance, and I appreciate that, because it shows that you have some comprehension of what acting, I mean, real acting is all about . . . But, I also think you have something to learn, and that is how to talk to a PPA . . . Post-Performance Actor. Now, listen, because I am not angry, and my feelings are not hurt, but I don't want our friendship to suffer simply because you are ignorant and don't know what to do because you haven't been told. Fred, there is no such thing as FCC . . . Friendly Constructive Criticism. That's hogwash. All criti-cism is destructive. The old FCC is an oxymoron presented by an oxyfool to an oxyfriend. Actors and actresses live lives of being criticized and believe me, Fred, it gets old. So, if you want to affect me, because you like me, then please use CCA . . . Constant Constructive Adoration. And, this simple and pleasant approach to actors can change your life. Now, do you want to grow as a person? Good. So, listen to me as I teach you the language of art. Stop squirming. It's only three words. Repeat after me.

"You are wonderful."

Come on. May I hear that, please?

"You are wonderful."

Once more.

"You are wonderful."

No. No. You're not trying. I want to hear the meaning of the words. And this time, try looking at me. Why? Because if you look at the wall, it means the wall is wonderful. Is the wall wonderful? No. I am. So, let's go. Okay? Again.

"You are wonderful."

That was terrible. Why are you having so much trouble? I know. Pretend you're my grandmother. Grandmother. Now:

"You are wonderful!"

Oh, that was better. See? You felt the difference. Now, again, but with real spirit.

"You are wonderful."

Nice. Now, get something in your eyes. Like you've just seen God. Okay? Once more. You are wonderful, from the top.

"You are wonderful."

Oh, yes!

"You are wonderful."

"Oh, no, I'm not. I'm good, not . . . Do you really think so?"

Damn it, Don't hesitate! Timing is crucial to belief. Try it again and don't stutter! Think grandchild! Think rainbow.

"You are wonderful."

Okay! That was better. That was very good. Again. Again. Again. Oh, nice. Very nice. Yes, I am wonderful. Oh, Fred, someday you'll thank me for this. Because not only are you becoming socially acceptable to the theatrical fraternity, but, guess what? You're also becoming a damn fine actor. Two more times and you may order dessert.

I'm very upset. Last night, I had another case of the threes. You know. You come home at midnight. Alone and restless. To what? To a room that's a closet, to a life that's a dump, to a building that houses every tense and chilling anxiety that you escape, at least to a certain degree, when you're in the streets doing something. But inside your little room, Anxiety Arms has you cold. I have to speak to someone. But, I can't. It's three o'clock in the morning. It's too late. It's not nice. It's too selfish—I—wait! My phone was ringing. Someone was calling me. Someone knew that I need help.

"Hello?"

I won't tell you her name, you probably know her. She's an actress. Here it is three in the goddamn morning, after three, and she's calling to tell me that she's considering suicide and that her skull is shrinking. And on and on. I can't even get in one word about myself, which I'm dying to do and then . . . click. Yes. Click! She puts me on hold. It's almost dawn and I'm on goddamned hold! What does that mean? Finally, she gets back on and says she can't talk to me now, she's got to speak to Rosalind. Rosalind? I'm not even primary rescue. She says:

"G'night, Ruth."

Ruth? I'm Yvette. And then, I realize she doesn't even know who she's talking to. How many people has she dialed? Oh, God. This hurts. Don't you see? In this game I'm just an amateur three, up against the pros! Actors. Are we all crazy? Is every actor in the world going through hell? Yes. So, why not just get a party line and have a hell call? Put us all together in one frenzied lump.

"I didn't get a callback. I'm up for an audition. I have a meeting. I need an agent. I'm killing myself. I'm leaving the business."

I'm so upset. I thought I was unique. But I'll never be. My head is one size. I'm garbage. Even my neuroses aren't worth a callback. Oh, man. And I had to pick up the phone.

I don't care about reviews. I don't! They don't affect me. What the hell does it mean? What the hell does it mean as long as I know I have done excellent work? I know and the audience knows. They're the ones who are paying. Okay, sometimes the audience doesn't know and if they don't, too bad; because if they don't know enough about what they are seeing to appreciate it, then it's not my fault. Let them learn. Because my co-actors know. They know the integrity of my work! And, if they don't get it, screw them. They measure me against themselves, but I know. And if I don't like what I've done, so what? What the hell do I know? We were doing *Under the Yum Yum Tree*, a fine play in Dilby, Georgia. Dinner theater. The show was solid. I was fabulous. Okay, I was damned good. So, here comes the local critic: Paul Pansy with his wife, the masochist in blue. Is it my fault if the food sucks? Is it my fault if he lives in Dilby? Is it my fault that Arlene spilled iced tea on him? I wish she'd spilled the whole goddamned buffet on his ugly, squashed, puny twisted little head. I can take criticism, but only when it's justified! Second-rate? Who are you calling second-rate? And PIDDLING? I'll give you piddling! I'll piddle on you! Long after I leave this dump and am piddling on Broadway, you'll be here because you'll be dead! Dead! I know voodoo. My aunt saw this production in New York and she knows excellence! And, what are your qualifications, fatso? What the hell have you ever done besides grow onions? Go back to your tractor! Keep plowing until you find a brain. You asshole! I can take criticism. Can you? Can you? CAN YOU TAKE IT? HUH? You . . . and, then the second critic shows up. Sarah Scumdrop. It must be his cousin. This is the only town in the world where the village intellectual and the village idiot are the same people. What's in the soil? STUPIDITY? Arlene, get me a gun!

Today, I had my third rejection this month. But, who cares? Because, I will make it. I was turned down for a role in a revival of *Equus*. A fine show. I was too old for the kid, too young for the psychiatrist, and too small for the horse. But I went anyway. And I was turned down. But, I will make it. Last week I auditioned for a ten-city tour of *The Pajama Game*. I can sort of sing, I can't dance; I wasn't right for any of the roles, but what the hell, I went anyway. I will make it. A month ago I was up for *Summer and Smoke*. I was perfect for that. I can play any of the roles. You know that. I gave a fabulous audition. Nothing. But, I am not discouraged. I'm not saying that I'm encouraged, either. But I did give two great auditions and I will make it. I will make it. I have a lot of talent. Everyone who's seen my work, knows that. I have ability. I will make it. I will make it. I will make it! I WILL make it. I WILL make it! I WILL make it! I am hungry. AND I WILL MAKE IT! OH, GOD, LET ME MAKE IT! I WILL MAKE IT! I WILL MAKE IT. I MUST MAKE IT! I WILL . . . MAKE IT! . . . and if I don't? So what. I'm not going to let it bother me.

We were up in Kennebunkport. After the Friday night performance, I'm sitting with Arlene in the crowded coffee shop, because we have been having our problems on stage and it's time to air it out. So I say:

"Put down the burger. If you want to tell me something, say it. I'm here. What?" And she says:

"Well, Jason, it's your performance. You're shouting."

"Of course, I'm shouting. I'm supposed to shout. I'm Stanley Kowalski. What should I do? Sing?" And she says,

"But, you shout during quiet moments. You shout when you kiss me!"

"My kiss is not a shout. My kiss is passionate!"

"Your kiss is a bellow. It's like necking with a bull. You shout when you say hello. It's not a greeting. It's a declaration!"

"I—"

"In Act Two, you don't enter. You invade. You say Hi, like you were goddamned Moses. There are other people in the play!"

"I know that."

"Then why don't you pay attention to us? You're on a stage! Not Echo mountain!"

"Look, if there's something wrong with my work, and I know there isn't, let the director tell me. He's very pleased with my performance."

"Of course he is. He's in love with you."

"He's in love with me? No. I thought he was in love with you."

"Are you kidding? Jack loves you! Everyone knows it."

"Would you mind not shouting?"

Every head in the place was looking at us.

"He loves you! That's why you were cast and he almost fired Cindy because he knows you love her and God, she's only sixteen!"

"She's eighteen!"

"She's not even seventeen! She's sixteen and she's a local. Grow up!"

I had to get out of there fast. I turned to the people next to us. Six townies.

"Just a scene we're rehearsing, folks. Enjoy your evening."

And I got the hell out of there.

I learned something. I learned. Never, ever, ever air it out in the only place in town that serves food after ten. And that's why I was hanging around the gas station when it was robbed and that's how come I lost my wallet and my best pair of boots. Sixteen? It's a good thing I found out. I was always afraid to ask. But, she is a great girl, and I will write to her. Summer stock. Man, this is dangerous.

God! I loved those boots.

Monologues. I had to find some monologues. I'd bought every goddamned book there is. Monologues by Mamet, Wilde, women, Williams, the best monologues of this year, last year, the last ten years, the first five years, the past three weeks. Many of them good, all of them done. But, I want to give them something they've never heard before and will never hear again. I want to knock the walls down. I want the job, man. Or, if not, at least when I'm finished I want them to know that they've seen a performance. So, this is what I did. I decided to write my own. Use what you know. So, my job at the time was in Telemarketing. Monologue grist? I think not. I'm trying to sell me, not light bulbs. So, I was about to audition and ready to fall back on my "Danny and the Deep Blue Sea." And then it hit me and on the spot I became for them a telephone surveyor on the job for twenty years who finally goes berserk in the middle of trying to con a blind man into buying a ten years supply of Halogen lamps. May I?

"No, don't accept them. No. No. Please, Mr. Krumsky, say no to bulbs!"

And, I go nuts. I start screaming names from two decades of computer print-outs; names of all the innocent people I had sold over-priced crap to. Don't you see? I am not only purging my soul, but, by God, I am doing it alphabetically.

"Ackerman, Beatrice. Agosto Carmelo, Addison M. I'm sorry. I'm sorry. Backenroth, Roberta, Bader, Jack Dr., Bharwani, Ravi."

And on and on, sobbing, wrenching. They say a good actor can make the telephone book interesting; hell, I was making it a saga.

"Tutsky, Henry, Tung King Wan, Tu . . . Lee . . . TYMAN, LEOPOLD B.!"

Overcome, I collapse in a heap of contrition and ultimate grace, slurring and drooling toward my final Z.

"Zuppacconi, R."

Incredible. Well, it must've taken ten minutes. They didn't even try to stop me. When it was over, the director, a very pale man, about forty, I think his name was Morton, asked me, after a long and deferential pause, if that was from a play. I lied: Yes. Because I don't want them to know that I can write. And then he came up to me and sort of hugged me and led me gently to the door, saying:

"Very nice. Really good work. Very different."

And, this has never happened to me before, but he actually slipped me a five dollar bill.

"Why don't you take a cab home?"

Which I think is a terrific compliment. It's the first time I've ever been paid for an audition. Have you? Anyway, I think it can use some cutting, but damn it, it worked. It really was cooking. Why? Because it came from within. That's the key. From within. And I'm going to use it again. Because I need something unique. And this time, I've got it. I think I've got a winner.

I had to call you. How's the show going? *Angels at Breakfast*? One of the great plays of the American theater? How can it be going? I'm playing Linda. A great role. The best woman's part in the play. It's been going beautifully. And then tonight; God. Oh, God. It's the scene in Act One. Maybe, my best work. My husband, Oedipus, has just gone off to the garage to whistle. I know he's going nuts. I'm worried. I'm his wife. I'm waiting for my son, Ziff. And I'm sewing. And, I'm waiting. And I'm sewing. And there is no Ziff. I'm alone on the goddamn stage, Ziffless! I have enough time to knit a quilt. I'm scared. And finally I look up . . . and it's not Ziff! It's his brother, Happy! The wrong son! Happy knows Ziff has blown his entrance, so he comes on to save the play. He starts doing Ziff's lines. What else can we do? As well as he can:

"What's Pop doing in the garage?"

Me: "Shh!" So far so good.

Happy as Ziff: "Gee whiz, Ma, has Pop popped his kernels?"

Me as Linda: "Quiet, he might hear you."

Happy as Ziff: "I didn't know he'd fallen quite this far."

And so on. And we're doing it. Yes! Five minutes. We're all the way up to my line: "July Fourth. Sixty dollars." And we're making it all work, when here comes Ziff! Pale as a ghost, having screwed the play that we have miraculously saved. And what does he say? You won't believe it.

Ziff: "What's Pop doing in the garage?"

Me: "Shh!"

Him:"Gee whiz, Ma, has Pop popped his kernels?"

You got it. NIGHTMARE! I'm now doing the same goddamned scene but with a different son while the first son is still there, listening to everything we just said! Happy, thinking fast, says:

"Hey, Ziff, funny how we think alike. You'd think we were brothers. Which we are! So, let's talk about something else."

So, now Ziff catches on and he starts to do Happy's lines, so that Happy can still do his lines.

So, now I have two sons who have switched identities! And no one knows what the hell we're saying! I'm doing their lines; they're doing my lines and I look into the wings and there's Eddie, stunned, looking out at two sons who are now each other! So, what does he do to help?

39

Nothing! He's waiting for his cue. What cue? I couldn't get there with a jet. So I, jumping totally out of sequence, shout:

"A cucumber doesn't have a heart!"

His cue. But, Eddie that jerk, doesn't move. So, then Ziff yells:

"A cucumber doesn't have a heart." And soon we're all yelling "A cucumber doesn't have a heart." And finally, Eddie walks on and the sons say: "Hi, Pop." and Eddie says to the real Ziff:

"Are you, Happy?"

And Ziff says,

"No. I'm not Happy anymore."

So, I say to the real Happy: "I want you to be Happy, again!"

And Happy says: "Mom, in MY heart, I've always been Happy."

And we get out of it. Ten minutes of acting hell. Hell. The people loved it. I don't think they knew anything was wrong. But, we did. We sure as hell did. I'll never be the same.

This happened. I met Paul Newman. Okay, I saw him. But, I really met him. I was going up to see about a temp job; receptionist for an insurance company at a building on West 56th street and I'm in the lobby and waiting for the elevator. YES! Paul! Next to me, in a coat, over a suit, and handsome, so handsome. I just stood there. He was like a foot away with another man. Well dressed, but boring. Paul and I. It was Paul and I in that elevator. Oh, recognize me, Paul. Look at me. Know that I'm an actress. He kept his fantastic eyes straight ahead. But, he knew that I was there. Oh, it's stupid and demeaning; what can he do for me? What can he say? But, he can see me! And that is almost enough. Just that. I want to scream: Here I am, Paul! Just say: Hi! Anoint me with a smile. Because we are the same. Both actors. I know what he's been through, and he knows me. You're a success and I will be. We have everything in common. Go slow, elevator. Stop on every floor. We need these moments to be together. I with my Paul. PAUL! PAUL! Notice me! Love me, take me off this elevator and into your next film, befriend and love and cherish me. Introduce me to your wife. I'll be cute. I'm not a threat. You need someone young. Paul, you smell good. You are me. You are famous. Dusty in tweeds, reliable and glass-eyed and God-like. Goddamnit, look at me. What are you? Blind? Wake up, Newman! You're no spring chicken! Do you know what you're missing? Twenty. He got off. What could I do? I followed. Was I crazy? The receptionist smiled up, a male receptionist, and I don't like male receptionists, they give me the creeps, and Paul walked through those imposing glass doors and away from me; swallowed up in a brief flash of light and I stood there, almost crying, really, almost crying, clearly and painfully on the wrong floor.

There's more to this. I got the job as the receptionist, and every day I would linger in the lobby, hoping, looking. I never saw him again. How many times can I go up and down in an elevator? I have my pride. But, what the hell is pride? I thought of leaving him a note, but I couldn't think of a reason why. Anyway, I felt touched. Encouraged. And more confident than I have ever been. Because, if he exists, then maybe I do, too? Thank you, Paul. Thank you, honey, my darling, for a really great day.

I was in my first movie. But, I almost died. I had just come back from Arkansas; *Murder at the Howard Johnson's*. Limited success, but I was good. We travel by train, sleepless. I get home at dawn, the phone rings at ten; it's my friend Bob, who is working on this movie, I didn't even know it. He's the producer's assistant. It's the new Robin Williams flick. They're doing a theater scene at the Playhouse Theater on 47th street; do I have a black suit, a tie and can I be there in an hour. You know where I live! Brooklyn. There is no transportation. "Bob, I'll be there."

So, I don't have a black suit, so I borrow my roommate's. He'll never know and I need a shower, screw that, and a shave, so I put my razor in my pocket, and I run out the door already deciding that there is no way to make it by train, so I trot the three blocks to Ocean Parkway and start to hitch; and who stops for me, a guy in an open jeep and I jump in and before we go six blocks, it starts to rain, not heavy, but a drizzle, and I tell him about the movie and he says: "For real? Don't worry, man. We'll make it."

And we do, but not before he cuts off a cab, is that an oxymoron? And the cursing was great and it's raining much heavier as we screech up to the theater, on time! And I reach my hand into my jacket pocket and manage, don't wince, to cut my thumb on the razor, so I run into the theater, through the stage door, in my wet suit, arm in the air, and blood running down my hand into my jacket sleeve, and they see me, and the next thing I know, I'm in a cab and I'm off to St. Luke's to get stitches because the cut is not bad, but it ain't great and the doctor an Indian guy when he hears that I have to be in a movie says: "Cinema? Oh, I love the cinema."

And everybody starts flying. Forms, sutures, shots. And I'm back at the theater thank God, less than an hour late, and I arrive running, but in the alley I slip and fall on my ass, so help me, in a puddle, in my friend's suit, in water so filthy it could eat a shark, Oh, man. But, in I go, fast as hell, and right on to the stage and all these great lights and what do I see? About two thousand actors in black suits. And they give me a seat number like one thousand six hundred eighty-four, and I'm in the last goddamned row. I'm on the moon. I'm an astronaut. And they don't shoot the scene for six hours, while I sit in my sewer-stink suit with my throbbing finger and my sore ass. I could have crawled from

Brooklyn.

I get paid about a hundred bucks for the day, but the hospital bill came to almost three hundred, plus the cabs and the dry cleaning; so I'm out about two hundred and a pint of blood. If I'm any more successful, I'll be dead. But, on the other hand, I loved working with Robin. It's a great credit. And if it turns out that I'm visible, well, go see for yourself.

I'm in the last row, but, I was very good.

I want to finish my comments by saying that a lot of the success I've had in my brief Off-Broadway career I owe to my training at this university and it's great to be back for a visit. Any questions? Yes? Young lady? How do I warm up? . . . What do you have in mind? Just kidding. You mean how do I prepare prior to a particular performance? It's very simple. I warm up with the Ten Commandments. Oh, not all of them. That would be ridiculous. Just a select few. Not for any particular religious reason. I just like them. Now, I'm not saying that this will work for you, but it does for me. No. I don't want to do them now. Suffice to say I used to caw. Caw! Caw! But, I started to sound like a bird. And I—Okay. I'll do a few. My favorite warm-up Commandments.

Thou shalt not commit adultery! Thou shalt not commit adultery. Ha! Ha! Thou shalt not commit adultery! Ha! Thou shalt not covet thy neighbor's wife! Thou shalt not covet thy neighbor's wife. Oh, yeah. Oh, yeah . . . Thou . . . well, you get the drift. It frees me. Oh, by the way, I may be doing a film with Dustin Hoffman, Gene Hackman and Gregory Peck, but it's too soon to talk about. Any other questions? How much money did I make last year. Well, I don't like to brag about those things. But, in the solid six figures . . . unfortunately, that includes cents. Listen, I don't want to give you the impression that I'm a huge success, but I'm working and I have made some big contacts with very important people. Questions? No, the last movie was not soft porn. One of those is enough. Well, let me finish by saying just a few years ago, guys, I was sitting where you are and now, look at me. Remember; work hard, don't despair, and meet people who can further your career. Oh, this afternoon, I'll be over in the cafeteria, hanging out, so if any of you want to come over and talk some more, particularly the girls, just kidding, just kidding, feel free. So, it's great to be back where it all started and thank you very much.

Let's talk money here because I'm an an actor and acting is a business, like it or not, and I am a professional. So, let's talk about the one word we all associate with money: Right. Family. You wanna be an actor? You wanna be a hit? Start laying the groundwork now. Get along with Mom and Pop. I come to New York, out of a terrific season of summer stock. *Kismet!* Do I have to say more? And my family, having seen me on stage, well, now they know what they have. Flash forward. Two weeks in New York. And, I'm hitting the wall of fiscal reality. Listen to this phone call and learn.

"Ma, it's called Equity, and I have to join otherwise there's no reason to be here! It costs only eight hundred dollars plus the thirty-nine for the dues, for six months . . . Is that bad?

"Ma, it's got to cost something. What's eight hundred thirty-nine dollars? Thank you. You're great. You'll get it back. Every penny."

Notice how I'm up front and to the point. These are my parents and I love them. And I will not trick them into anything.

"Ma, Equity means new pictures. I can't use the old ones. I look like I'm twelve. Photographer, prints, mailing, follow-up; no more than five hundred dollars. And that's rock bottom and worth every penny. What happened to what money? I spent it. Okay, so you paid for the plane tickets, but I had to eat. Put Dad on. He just left?"

See how I did that? No con job about being mugged! I had money. I spent it. I tell the truth! Because I am an actor and I have dig—

"Ma, stop screaming. Ma, please. I promise I will never call you again and ask for money . . . That's why I have to tell you right now about something called SAG. Screen Actors Guild. One thousand twelve dollars and fifty cents. Ma? Ma? Are you there?"

It takes guts to go for all of it in one shot but I am a man. These are my parents. I love them too much to nibble them to death.

"So, all in all, the whole thing doesn't even come to much more than five thousand dollars which is a lot less than you'd spend to open a business! Right? Or buy a car? Why do you need a car?"

In one week, the money was there.

Being an actor isn't cheap. Oh, it costs. It costs in the doubts that people have, it costs when your brother gets his masters, and you have nothing, it costs when you go home for Thanksgiving; and they look at you. Oh, that really costs. And it costs in the waiting and fear that sometimes turns inward and scares you to death. Jesus, I may never succeed. Damn. Not only may I not succeed, but I'll owe over five thousand dollars . . . and college! Being an actor isn't cheap. But, let me tell you something: Being anything else would cost me even more.

Wait'll I tell them about my teeth.

"Did you enjoy the show? Really? Why, thank you very much. Oh, we love being in Virginia. It's a beautiful state. Did you really enjoy the show? No, I have been in other plays. Did you read the program? Why, thank you. Thank you, very much. Well, after here we go to Pine Hill for a month. Oh, you have friends there? What's it like? Like here, but, a little smaller? Good. No, we remember all the lines. Honest. Nothing is written on the stage. Did I wait on you? I thought you looked familiar. Thank you. I beg your pardon? Your roast beef wasn't rare? Oh, I'm sorry. How was . . . No, the desserts are homemade. Thank you."

WE JUST BROKE OUR ASSES FOR TWO HOURS AND SHE HATED THE ROAST BEEF! We did two hours of one of the finest if not the funniest productions of *Under the Yum Yum Tree* ever done anywhere and all they leave here with is indigestion and pockets stuffed with biscuits! You sons of bitches! I want to shake you. Take us home. Take us. Because this was acting, not gastronomy. You understand? Digest us! Fill your bellies and your guts with ours. Know what the hell you've seen, and next time pour your own goddamned iced tea and fucking decaffein—defaffeinated coffee. POUR IT! YOU BASTARDS! I know they're nice people. I know they're nicer than I am. And, if I was a human being I'd want to be just like one of them. But, I'm not. I'm an actor! Oh, God, I'm an actor and I can't stand real people. Roast beef. That's what I am. I'm a roast beef. I'm sorry. I get this way. I'll be okay tomorrow. I will. Jesus Christ! Is there anywhere within ten miles that doesn't close at nine? PINE HILL IS SMALLER THAN HERE! You may send me back to New York in a bag.

Here it is. I told you that in this class, I would tell you how to be a successful actor. I promised that I would go beyond the normal scene work and the over-used textbooks and give you all something invaluable. Students, I am ready to share with you my acting secret . . . Eyeballs! Eyeballs. Eyeballs. That's all you need to know. Why eyeballs? Remember, the audience isn't always listening, but sometimes, they might be watching! So, even if you goof up, they'll never know, if you use what? E.E. Eyeball Excitement! Quick. Someone give me a line. Quick. Okay. I'll make one up. Something bland, something impossible. Here. Are you having a nice day in Alaska? A challenge.

"Are you having . . . a nice day in Alaska?"

Did you see that? Did you see my left eye? Did you see what I did? The left one. I took a perfectly innocuous line and made it into something exciting. Okay, maybe that was a bad example. Give me a line. Any line. Good. The lamb chops are in the freezer? Terrific. Static, boring and frozen. Watch me. Watch.

"The lamb chops . . . are . . . in . . . the freezer."

Okay? Did you see? Of course, it was subtle. That's my art. Thank you. Did you see that move? How could you miss it? Total eye excellence! Now, I'm telling you this much, and nobody else I know teaches this in any acting school on the Eastern seaboard; Rule number one: Don't be an idiot and wear glasses on stage, even rims! It can ruin your performance. I don't care what the director says! You fight for your eyes! What we are doing, class, is giving the people something extra and unexpected. You are giving them . . . THE EYE! You are creating precious eye moments. Four or five of those in a play and you are something special. Oh, and of course, I'm also referring to the eyebrow. It's a package. I mean, I am talking here about total retinal commitment for real ocular excellence. Now, kids, that's all I'm going to say today. This stuff is almost oriental in its concept, so you cannot expect to have the techniques mastered in less than two or three years. And, we'll be going back to it in future classes. Now, I'm an eyeball actor, but, and this is not in my book, I knew an actress who was mostly tongue. Those roots are Balkan. You had to see her work. We did the Cherry Orchard. It was . . . it was . . . magnificent. She began so slowly; incredibly deft, but by the end of Act Four her tongue-work was so brilliant that everyone in the cast, and the audience, was enthralled. What ideas. Her last line, and I can't even come close to her, but . . .

"Mama, Mama, the train. Hurry, or we'll miss it."

Did you see? Tongue everywhere! Outside her mouth, yes, but always in character and by doing that: transcending character! That, my friends, is acting! Mark my words. If I teach you nothing else, learn this: An actor with good eyeballs and a working tongue can almost always make a living. Especially, and don't put it down, in beer commercials. Now, next week, we review seawater so bring your equipment and just a reminder, we're enrolling now for next semester. Time flies. Alice has the list. Thank you.

I'm an actress waiting for a call-back. So, if you want to live just stay away from my phone. I'm waiting. Ring, baby, ring. I sit. I wait. Y'know, if I could teach a course to actors on how to wait for the phone to ring, I'd be so rich, I wouldn't have to act! Why are they doing this to me? They said they would call before six. And, I've been waiting since WAYYYY before six. Think about men. Food. Or both. Nothing works. Right now, my entire body is one, huge goddamned ear. Y'know, I think every actress, in her career, has this Tantric revelation: My telephone is life. IT'S LIFE! Cement my mailbox, burn my resume, eat my cat, but don't you dare touch my AT&T. They said they would— Wait! Oh, my God? Is it working? It hasn't rung for hours. Should I lift it up to check the dial tone? Or run to a pay phone to hear it ring? But, what if, just then, they call? I won't be here! They'll hire someone else and my career will be over.

"She's not there. She must not have wanted the part. And she would have been perfect. Too bad. Who's next?"

No one is next! I'm here! I—It's FIVE TO SIX! I'm dying. I know. In fifteen minutes, I'll call them. Yes.

"Hi. You won't believe this, but I've been out all day, and there's been something wrong with my answering machine." Yeah, sure. They'll laugh in—wait! Ringing! Oh, it's ringing.

"Hello? . . . Hello?"

I don't believe this. There's no one there. It was the curse of the waiting class: a one-ringer. Who was it? DON'T TORTURE ME! Come on, you red-plastic son of a bitch! Ring or I'll take this cord and twist your guts out. Please. You dialed my number, you were interrupted. Don't give up . . . I'm waiting . . . Well? It's not ringing. I can't take much more. I tell you, if I was dead, and laid out cold, peaceful in the parlor, and the phone rang, I'd have a resurrection so fast and so furious, they'd need to schedule two Easters . . . It rang, you heard it! But, now IT'S NOT RINGING! And I'm supposed to live with dignity? I'll call them. No. I won't. Fine. Have it your way. So what? I have a life. I am a full person with a full life. And, there are other roles in many other plays. It's after six . . . I'm dead . . . Enough. I'm going out. Oh, God, I wish I had something to eat. I am starved.

I enrolled in the Academy. First, I auditioned. I was accepted. So, I took theater craft, stage craft, space identity, basic movement. I want to act. I took advanced movement, stage combat, phonetics, costume design and set building. So, I built flats, stretched canvas, glued flats, spackled and smelt glue and ruined several pairs of pants. I want to act. I did scene shop, and costume shop and prop shop. I sewed, stitched, vented, bitched, pleated, bleated, hemmed and hawed. I took stage managing. I railed, failed, led and bled, made prop lists, call lists, rehearsal lists, and made two lists of missed lists. I want to act. So, I took theater history, scene study, mime, stage craft two. Space identity again, because I flunked it the first time, basic directing and the structure of the fucking Siamese one-act play. I want to act! Is that wrong? I took preparation, separation, desperation, hesitation, flirtation, aggravation, condemnation, gesticulation and self-flagellation. Speculation, gyration, and god damned damnation. Damn it! I can do that part! I can. I want to act! Act! Act! Act! Act! My final semester was PRIVATION! FRUSTRATION! AND DISINTEGRATION! Otherwise, I made some real good friends and had a great three years. Thank you. But, you won't see me at our ten year reunion, because it might take me twenty before I get a job. Thank you and good night.

I'm thinking about giving up my career. Seriously. I know I have talent. But, talent isn't enough. Luck is very important. And who you know. And I know a lot of other people. But, they don't seem to know me. And if I leave and go back, it will be with no regrets. No, that's a lie. I will regret having never made it. The business wears you down. The men. The constant rejection. The occasional crumb. Looking for a boyfriend. Hoping that he's not crazy. I live in Buffalo, New York. I can get a job. I can finish college. I have two boyfriends to choose from and I'm not even there. I don't want my life to go by without a home. Family. Children. A car. And I know I'll get married and be close to my sisters, and cousins, who still live there with their kids and their cars.

It will be a very difficult trip. A train too slow, a plane too fast. And, I'll be there. Just like that. Back. And, I'll be married. And everything will follow as it should. And . . . And watching my children grow and my husband age, and my parents die, and my hair grow gray, and my job or jobs, and social work in Buffalo, and teaching in Buffalo, and the church group in Buffalo, all these things, all good, all fine, but I will always have had this time in New York, and, then Buffalo Community theater, and I'll be damned good, and directing the teenagers at the church, but, I still will have had this time in New York, and no matter how many noses I wipe, and no matter how many floors I wash in Buffalo, or charities I help, or snow I see in deadly quiet afternoons, chewing time to shreds in elongated phone calls to my husband, to my sisters, to my friends; and their friends, to relatives and their friends, I will have always had this. In this time I was me! And even though I may leave it, even though I couldn't take it, even though I had to go back to myself and to everyone who knows I didn't make it, up in Buffalo, they knew I wouldn't make it when I left, but I didn't know. How could I? How could I possibly know? But, this I knew then, and know now. No matter the place, the day or the minute. No matter the subject of the day, the color of the car, or the name that's on the door . . . I will always be an actress, always, and I will always have New York.

The following monologues have to do with a particular imaginary production. They are meant to be done individually, but can also be done sequentially for group work in a class.

The idea came to me slam-bang. Original? Not at all. But it could be if I did it right. I'm an actor. In New York. Two years, I'm getting nowhere. Who is? A few people are; luck. They have it, I don't. So, I decide, if you can't be them; be them!

Do you get my idea? Form my own theater group!

What can it possibly take? Every dope does it. I know the people, I have the talent. I know the desire. Oh, how I know the desire. So, it takes about twenty phone calls, no less, and I wind up with seven beside myself. Two losers, three roses, two semi-lemons and I arrange our first meeting. At my place. Simply put: The most brilliant night of my life. I am so sterling. I begin low key and almost meaning what I say.

"Blah, blah, blah. BLAH!" I'm doing fine.

"And so, we all came to New York to act. But, are we acting actors? Or are we merely actors merely acting at being actors? Simply put, are we doing what we want to do?"

And to my amazement four of these idiots say yes, ruining my rhythm. But I've been on stage long enough to know how to cover.

"Okay, let's cut the crap. Words take time. This is the point. We're all selfish. I am. You are. Who isn't? What do we want? Good plays! And what's a good play? One with big fat roles for us! Why? Why not? But, anybody can do theater. And who doesn't? But, if you join me, not us. Because we will do special stuff. The other day I misspelt theater. Know what I got? . . . Threat! And that's what we'll be. Threatening. I don't care if we stink, because if we stink, it will be with a special brave stench; because in this room my nostrils quiver with the strong odor of your raw talent. Take a bow. And who knows how long we'll last? We'll open with love and die with hate, subdivide or even vanish completely from each others lives. I know the game. But until then, we will act in some damned fine theater the way it's rarely done: with integrity, creativity, and most of all: USivity! Us!"

This was easier than I thought.

"I need you. We all need . . . each other."

After that, naturally, the rest of the meeting was just mopping up. We were a group. Actors. I'm one. Problemed, anxious, greedy, and yearning. We are going to do a play. Theater! Theater! God! THEATER! Oh, boy, Y'know, I can hardly wait to see what we do.

54

This is how an actress thinks.

I got this great phone call. It was from Ed. He was very excited. He pretended to be cool and mature. Which he is not. Ed's an actor. He was starting this new theater group and he wanted me. Well, he didn't just want me; I had to be in it. Was I available? Was I ready to change my life? I said maybe. This is how an actress thinks. I don't like Ed. Who does? But, what the hell? It's only bus fare. So I went to his apartment. Things were neat. Everyone was there. I knew four. Charlie Beede, who gained ten pounds and looked it. What a gut. Anita Druck, who was okay in *Madwoman* but in *Miss Firecracker* . . . fizzled. Yvette from Williamstown who obviously decided against surgery; a big mistake. And Marnie Lewis; talented, but, I'm better looking. Because, this is how an actress thinks. This is how an actress must think. What am I supposed to do? Join a group in which I'm the least of the lowly? Hell, no. But, why join at all? What good can possibly come of this bunch of acting school migrants? Who's going to come and see us? Our friends? We have no friends! Except for other out of work actors who'll hate everything we do anyway! But, this is how an actress thinks . . . and I'm an actress . . . Do you know how I think? Okay, I'll tell you how. I'll even tell myself. I want to act. That's it. I want to act. To hell with withering with class. I want that stage. The truth is I'd rather die acting, swallowed up in a group of bums; aging in makeup, shining in attempt, aglow in crap, than live a long life of waiting for something that's good enough for me. Proper vehicle? Come on! For my career, it's a hearse. I've been in more bombs than uranium. Oh, Jesus Christ. Just let me. Let me. Let me do it! This is how an actress thinks. Is it thinking? Does love know? Do instincts care? Do they really give a fuck about a goddamned resume? Well, do they? And, tell me this; is it worth bus fare to stay alive?

Well, let me tell you we had our second meeting of Ed's itching actors . . . EVERYONE WAS THERE! Do you hear me? EVERYONE! Which has to be a first and that's just one of many surprises. Let me get right to it. We chose our first production, and I knew, at least I thought I knew what Ed was up to, choosing a play that would give him a great role. We boiled it down to three. *The Insect Comedy*. Whose idea was that? A cast of flies and beetles? I want to thrill an audience, not bite them. *The Visit:* too serious, big cast; a powerful but dated drama, which I would be great in, and *Death of a Salesman* which Ed was fighting for and I was totally against because I knew what that phoney was up to. Don't con me, Mister Leading Man, I know your kind. Then came bombshell number one!

Ed wants me to play the lead! Me do Willy Loman. He would be glad to play Biff, but the girls were pissed because there's only one good part for a woman, Linda; the suffering wife. But Ed dropped bombshell number two! The role of the second son, Happy could be changed to a girl! We'd call her Snappy. An impossible idea. Outrageous. Why not? Screw it! Is Arthur Miller going to come? Then the debate started, but hell it didn't last! When it came right down to it, no one gave a damn as long as we could get good roles. Claire would be Linda and Yvette would be Snappy, once a son, now a daughter. Then Jason The Jealous said, "Why don't we just cut out all the characters and call it *Death* and next year we could do *The Icegirl Cometh* or *Hatful of Snot*?" Crude. Eat your liver, Jason. You jealous pig. It is settled. I, big, fat Charlie, am going to do Willy Loman! I am. It's a stretch. A real reason to act and right now, I'm excited and eager and, you know me, already worried. Ed has a director whom none of us know, and we start rehearsals next week. This is why I act, my friends. This is why! Oh, how I want this. I want this part. Ed? Could I have been wrong about you? Ed! My man!

Oh, let his sinks simmer, let his bathroom swoon with mysteries of algae, let his weak manners die at a whim, Ed wants me to play Willy. He knows I can act! He knows I can cut it and cut it big and I will not let him down. I didn't sleep that night. Today, I ran and bought the script. It's so good. I memorized my first page and felt better, really good and excited to be me; to be me an actor, an actor and I'm acting in New York.

Ed wants committees. I knew as soon as the phone rang it was bad news. I knew it. It was Ed with another of his stupid ideas. I hadn't heard from him in three months. I thought I was safe. "Let's start our own theater company." He needs some great actors and I'm a great actor. I asked him how many he saw in the group and he said about eight and I thought at least I might be able to meet someone new, someone with talent, but naturally, I knew five and never wanted to see any of them again, but I went. Out of curiosity, out of boredom and, because he begged. Well, close to it. And, of course, it was the most idiotic meeting I'd ever been to and I've been to some beauts.

Ed wants committees. Mister Organization man, Mr. Far-sighted Entrepreneur wants committees. Committees of what? You ASSHOLE! THERE ARE ONLY EIGHT PEOPLE HERE! What do you want? Twelve committees with half a person on each? I can't take it! Eight actors in one room is three above the legal limit. I want to shake them by the throats and shout:

"Maybe the reason why we're not all famous or rich is that we really aren't that damned good? Did you ever think of that?" Did you ever think? Committees? Long-range projections? Ha! How about some potato chips, Mr. Big? How about one goddamned ashtray, Mr. Hurok? You, Ed, with a bathroom that howls? You will create vibrant theatre? You, who has all the pent-up originality of two-week-old termite shit?! You? I'm sorry. I just . . . From committee chaos we next focus on the plays we want to do for our upcoming season. SEASON? God. Only actors bewitched by the alchemy of frustration can turn absolutely nothing into expectation. I want to get paid. Should I drop out now? Or, hang around? Stay until Ed loses his mind completely, until everyone hates everyone, until I see group number 712 die its own deserved, thudding death? Oh, what's the use? What's the use? People toy with actors. Even actors toy with actors. And I resent it. It's as if we're the world's designated yo-yos. Oh, I know other people go through what we go through. No, they don't! No one does. We meet again next week at his place again, said the control freak. Remind me to have my coffee and vaccines before I get there. And we left, all of us already trying to avoid each other. Leaving high, as if something great was achieved. Seven dreamers trooping down the stuffy hallways and out into the West Side street. Each pretending to go in different directions.

"Good night . . . Goodnight . . . Goodnight. Call me. Think about a name. Think about plays. G'night. Good night."

I mean, what the hell. You never know, do you? I mean, who knows? The frustration, the pain, the wonder is, we never really know. But, they know we're always here to try. "G'night. Good night . . ."

I've always liked Ed. He's talented and he is sexy. I don't mean he's good-looking, he's not bad-looking, wiry; I like that kind, forget fat, but he has personality, call it drive. I mean he's one of these actors who confuses energy, with talent. So, when he called with his idea about creating an acting company I didn't even pretend I was busy, I went. Besides me, he had six other sources of joy. It was a great first meeting. Very exciting. All that enthusiasm and discussion. And a lot of physical kneading and subverted body inspection. Hey, anytime you mix eight actors in a room, the agenda may be professional, but the subtext is immediately genital. And I like that. I watch it all. And I get involved. Ed started with a moving opening speech that gave me time to check out Jason who's been lifting weights, and brought to the meeting a very nicely developed upper-body, but it was soon Walt who gained my attention with a pair of tight jeans that outlined his precocious manhood. I caught Claire checking it out, too. So I concentrated on Ed, because I didn't want him to realize that he was being upstaged in his own apartment by another actor's penis. During "Play Selection" Jason, sitting across from Claire, began squirming in his chair to get a better look up her dress. She knew it and slyly kept it alive. It's a meeting. What else should we do? Ed was now on to directors, even as his glance kept shifting to Yvette's bosom. Ed used, "I say we bring someone in, naturally, because if he's a real director he might cast us someday in something else" to slide behind Yvette and begin rubbing her shoulders. Walt made a statement as a pretense to place his hand on my knee. The meeting was going well. Now, the topic was "Name The Company" and we literally began groping for answers.

Ed wanted "Blue Moon," using his enthusiasm to propel him to Claire so he could squeeze her arms and touch her neck. Nice move . . . I said "Power Play" (isn't that good?) which enabled Jason to lean over and rub my shoulder; touch my knee and my hip. Good one. Yvette suggested "Stage Screw" thus allowing Ed to dive back for a rewarding hug and a hand down the spine rub. I see it all. The minutes of the meeting: In under half an hour, we'd had eleven squeezes, fourteen thigh or shoulder pats, at least twenty overt crotch stares, and from the straight men nearly a hundred covert to overt breast evaluations and can-I-see-her-brassiere-strap-under-her-sleeve peeks. And this was without beer or wine! This could work out after all. I was psyched. I don't remember too much about what we talked about. At the door, I gave Ed an extra look, why not? and a little hand squeeze. And he, while always looking at someone else, dropped his hand, quickly down to my rump. And so we departed, most of us moderately massaged either by hand or eye, and what more can one expect? I think it was a terrific meeting with time well spent.

I'm upset. We're doing *Death of a Salesman,* that relic, and I'm the whore. I would say hooker, but that's not the mood I'm in. Why am I always the one who puts out for a pair of stockings? Why? Ten lousy lines. Is it my ass? Is it? What the hell has happened to my career? I went to Catholic school! I mean, God, give me a break. I don't want to do it. I don't care. If Ed, our producer, has the guts to change the part of Happy, the son, to Snappy, a daughter, for Yvette whom he has the hots for, he can do something for me. You know how they say there are no small parts only small actors? Wrong-O. There are small parts and there are very small actors, and I am small and mean and getting smaller. I mean it. The time and money I have spent and the care and the gym and love I have for my craft, never mind Mom and Dad; in addition to the one hundred ten dollars we're all supposed to fork over for dues. One hundred ten dollars. Why? So that Claire Short can be the wife while I get ten crappy lines? Is it my ass? Why? Why wasn't I born with the ass of an ingenue? No! I have to have this one. So, I called Ed. He actually answered the phone. And I gave it to him.

"Look, Ed, I'm not pleased. No. Let me speak. If you're making Happy, Snappy why can't Biff be Beatrice? Beatrice Loman! Let Willy have two daughters. One was adopted! Why not? Instead of football she could bowl. I'm not going to be a hooker! I want to play Beatrice. I can do Beatrice. I am Beatrice."

He said, "Anita, calm down. I was just going to call you." (Sure.) "I had to do it this way . . . strategy. Because, by doing *Salesman* with you as the woman, which is a very fine role, I am opening it up for our next production . . . *Romeo and Juliet*! And who's Juliet? You, babe! Me, Romeo. You the Julie girl! Okay? Lesser roles in this show, so we can nail them when it counts. We meek shall inherit the stage. Okay?"

Juliet? Oh, yes. I can do Juliet. I may have to lose a few pounds but I can do it. Ed is always up to something. I mean, I don't like strategies and con games and I don't like to be petty, but after five years in New York and all that I've gone through, sometimes that's all that's left. Oh, man. I can do Juliet! Wait. Is she a hooker? No. Okay, I'll play a hooker, just one more time, so I can get what I want. No, what I deserve. Sadly, for a woman or an actress this seamy strategy is probably not brand new. In fact, it's pretty brand old. But, THIS IS THE LAST TIME! . . . I hope.

I'm off and I'm running. I'm producing a show which I am in, and what an education. First of all, they always say that an actor makes choices. Baloney. An actor just does his best. How is that a choice? But, it's the producer who really makes choices. First, I chose the people. Then I chose the play. *Salesman*. A pretty safe piece of crap. Then I chose to give the lead to someone else. Why? Because they all would have said, "Come on." Hey, I can play Willy and brilliantly, at that. But, as producer I chose to keep Charlie happy because I hate him. I mean eight weeks in summer stock in Arkansas with him talking about himself seventy-five hours a day and reading aloud from *U.S. News and World Report* and you know this man's an asshole. But he has some talent and he will bring people. A choice. He knows agents. As the lead he'll bring them, and what am I doing this for if not to attract people to see me? And then I won over the women by making Happy a girl. What a move. I'm as good as Merrick. Okay, I know we're taking certain liberties with the script, but what is theater about if not liberation? I mean, what the hell is this: a play or The Bill of Rights? And then I had to handle Anita by making a whole thing about doing *Romeo and Juliet* next. Wow. As an actor I never could have lied that fast. And, now I even like the idea. I'm telling you, producing is inspirational. I've lied as much in the past week as I did in years of acting and with far better results. And I'm enjoying it. I love lying and everyone is saying "yes" to every wild thing I say. Oh, what a feeling. Now, all I have to do is find a director who's as desperate as we are, and I could really have a future. Power. Girls love it. The producer is in the room! And when they stand next to me, they lean a little closer. Why? I know why. Simply put: I am the producer. And that was my choice. You see, actors are dwarfs. How do I know? Because I'm an actor. We don't make choices. We are chosen. You, you . . . and you! I love it. Is this great? I don't know what my next choice is going to be, but I'm very eager to make it, because I have a feeling it's going to be something historic.

What a great bunch of people. What a great bunch. Ed Shray is
starting this new acting group and I'm in it. And I've got several lines in
his first production. I am so lucky. I can't stand it. There are nine of us
altogether. Four other girls besides me. We are doing something called
Death of a Salesman. I'm not supposed to tell you; with women playing
men's parts and other great ideas. I only just got to New York and it's
only costing me two hundred twenty dollars to join which when you
think about it is more than I would spend for acting lessons and it's
bound to be worth it. I went to their second meeting. It was so exciting.
At twenty-two I'm the youngest one there with all these experienced
and mature actors. They are calling themselves Group Ace Productions
which I think is so cool and Ed is just amazing. He chose me when he
saw me standing at the billboard at Drama Bookstore. I was looking for
a place to live. When I told him that, he said: "You may not have found
a place to live, but you just may have found a life."

What a line! Just dumb enough to be intelligent. He said he saw me
and something clicked. I hope it wasn't his fly. I think Ed likes me,
although I know he's almost thirty, but I think Jason and Walt like me
too, from the looks I was getting, but I can handle that. I can handle
anything right now. I suppose I should have my doubts; but I don't.
Everyone seems so nice. Since, I'm also going to be working some tech,
Ed wants to have a meeting with just him at his place. I think I can trust
him and besides it can't be as bad as the guy who wanted me to do a
love scene with him for his hand-held videocam. Please. Which he was
going to send to his partner Ed McMahon on *Star Search*. What a jerk.
Gee, one month in New York, just one month and I'm already part of
something. Ed was telling me his plans about developing young talent
and producing films. It sounds almost too good to be true. And I may be
moving in temporarily with Yvette who's in the cast. Ed said I could
crash on his couch, but I don't think so. Claire gave me advice.

"Polly, as an actress you simply must believe the obvious lies.
Because where are you going to get, if you don't?"

Is that great advice, or what? Anyway, I'm so happy. Ohhh.
Owww. Because as of today, I am an actress. A real honest-to-God
actress in a real New York production. Am I lucky? I am.

More than two weeks is enough. I can't be blamed. The relationship between an actor and his director is incredibly complex and important. It is so delicate. Here I am playing Willy Loman in a classic and my director is some know-it-all putz named Lance Von Cleeter. Two names aren't enough! This nitwit has to waste three. As soon as I saw the pipe jutting out of his stupid jawbone, the alarms went off! PEDANT! I know them. I know them all. College-major no-talent! CLEAR THE DECKS! You pipe-sucking, cardiganed simian! Props are nothing but excuses for insights. Leave the ascot at home and bring a brain! I'm on the goddamned stage, baby. I'm out there. Help me. I mean, I don't need to finish a rehearsal so that my director can say to me:

"Well, what do you think?"

What the hell does that mean? I'm an actor. I don't direct. You're the director. You get paid to think. THINK!

"Well, Charlie, why don't you try it again?"

Try it how, shmuck? Slower. Faster? Glibly? Globly? Do I go here? Or there? Or should I fly? Am I Willy Loman or Goddamned Peter Pan? WHAT THE HELL DO I DO? Ed, our producer playing Biff, saw I was a trifle upset and so was he, so we all stepped into the hallway to discuss our situation. Lance Von Cleeterballs said:

"Charlie, what's the problem, kid?"

"Well," I said, "Lance, kid, my problem is, that you stink."

"Charlie, I like to allow an actor to go through a process." And I said:

"And, I'd be happy if you went through a blender. You and your stupid pipe. And I'm only saying these things, because I hate you, you stupid dinner theater semi-faggot!"

"Charlie—"

"You're not a director! You're a waiter! Go away and get napkins!" The first punch he threw caught me pretty good. The rest is a blur. I remember fighting back. Using my arms and legs. There was a lot of screaming. The three of us wound up on the floor. But, in the tradition of great leading men, I never stopped punching. Lance resigned. So, now, with three weeks to go, we have no director and everybody in the cast is very upset. But, I don't care. Because, as I said, the relationship between an actor and his director is the game. It's everything! DOESN'T EVERYBODY KNOW THAT? So, give me a director who can or stay the hell out of my life and let me work!

Directors are not that important to a show. The actors usually come up with the best ideas, anyway. We're doing *Death of a Salesman*. My first director refused the project when he found out I was casting Happy as a girl. Screw him. Esthete. Purist. One thing you don't need in a low-budget production is a pile of stale ethics. So, I got Lance Von Cleeterman. A bad choice. His credits were as an inverse to his talent. So Charlie and Lance duked it out. My shirt was torn and I actually caught an elbow under my eye. The screaming was passionate. Von Cleeterman left the show. I felt bad, but thank God, I never paid the prick. And naturally, the next day everybody was going crazy because we had no director. So what? What the hell is wrong with actors? They hang on to a director's behind like barnacles to a boat's bottom.

"Director?" I scream at them. "Who cares? What we need is doors!"

"But—"

"Friday is set building day, and we have nothing to set with!"

"But, who's going to direct—?"

"Oh, stop. We're going to have an audience, right? Are they going to notice that there's no director? But, they'll sure as hell notice that we have no doors! When you come on stage, how many directors are you going to open? Let me worry about the stupid director, you worry about doors. Who has one?"

"Doors?" asked Anita.

"Yes. I mean like on your closet. You'll get them back."

The fact is New York is loaded with bad directors. Every building has at least two, but good doors are at a premium. Now, I toyed with the idea of doing the entire play with no furniture, just the old black boxes and bed sheets routine. Hackneyed. Quote me: Impressionism is just an other word for cheap. I want doors. As many as I can get. And some furniture. I thought I had some great stuff off the street until the people moving in came after me with a lamp. I told them I would give them credit in the program, but they wouldn't understand. So, quote me: If I can't get good furniture I'll settle for more doors. A friend of mine did *Streetcar* in Illinois with nothing but doors. The set meant nothing, but it was cheap and the critics loved it. After all, this is New York's first Ed Shray production. And, goddamn it, it must have an Ed Shray "look." Am I right? AM I RIGHT? I'm going for . . . SOMETHING! Thank you.

Without a doubt this is the worst goddamned production of anything that I have ever been in anywhere! We're doing *Death of a Salesman* with six different directors! All of them us! WHAT IS THIS? I am suffering. The leading man punched the director in the mouth so he quit. Why? Is it the first time you've been punched during rehearsal? Okay. So, get another one. But no, our producer Ed the Empty comes up with this classic boner: If you're not in a scene, you can direct it. You heard me. I am not making that up. I wish I was. It's Russian roulette. A smorgasbord of shmucks. And pardon me for being vulgar, because I am not normally, but I am no longer normal. The classic *Death of a Salesman* coming at you in several distinct styles. Oh, goody. Claire, the asshole, and I never curse a woman, unless I'm dating her, but there is no other word, has decided that Act Two needs more fun. Fun? What the hell does she think this is? The Comédie Fucking Française? THIS IS A GREAT DRAMA! So, Walt the Wonderdog, decides to direct my scene, my best scene, by telling me to play Ben the ghost, with a funny accent and a rash.

"Excuse me? A RASH? Why?"

"Because. Jason, don't ask why, try it!"

"No, I will ask why. I have every right to ask why."

"Because, you've been to Africa, haven't you?"

"And that's a reason for a rash?"

"It could be."

So, now I sound like Boris Karloff who found everything in Kenya except calamine lotion. But, I will get my revenge. I am directing the Wonderdog in his scenes! He's Bernard, the little jerk next door, good casting, so I say,

"Walt, I want you to play Bernard as a latent homosexual, who, and here's the surprise, is not hot for Biff, but who harbors a secret love for Willy Loman! Biff's fat, ugly father."

HE LOVED IT! THEY ALL DID! Now, Bernard is acting with a lisp. I say: "Latent! Not blatant! And take off the goddamned rouge!" They all think it works. I hate life. When I was in college I was excellent. I played Oedipus. Everyone thought I was six foot five. And I was. Oh, I was. You have to believe me. I was. If only you could have seen me in that. If only you could have seen me. What's going to happen to us? They're inviting people. I'm getting very nervous. What's going to happen?

I admit I was inspired by Jason, who is playing Ben, but directing Walt as Bernard. I'm doing Linda in *Death of a Salesman*. The dishrag wife. Good-hearted, good-hearted, good-hearted. But, I was having trouble finding a character. Why is this woman so good-hearted? Because she still loves Willy Loman? Oh, come on! He's a tub. A half-lunatic, fat failure who's been screwing hookers in Boston for thirty years. So, why am I still there? I know. Because I have a powerful driving lust for Biff, my son! That's why I want him home! Screw Willy! It's Biff. So, we're rehearsing the scene in Act One where Biff says:

"All right, pal, all right,"

and leans over to kiss Mommy goodnight. But, this time, I leap to my feet and grab him by the neck and sear him with a soul-shocking, tooth-melting kiss tight on his mouth, with hips pressed and spinning on his, while my hands palpate his ass. Wow! You want a moment? STUNNING! The look on his face. Theater! Pow! Well, when I let him go, all hell broke loose. Charlie was cheering. Walt was leering. Anita approved, but the best was Ed, who plays Biff, shaking me briskly by the shoulders:

"Are you crazy? You can't kiss me! You're my mother!"

And I say: "I know! Haven't you ever heard of *Hamlet*?"

Anyway, a lot of the tension of the past few weeks blows up and we have a good shouting match. Everyone is in it! And, I stand my ground, defending my choice.

"Why can't Linda get lucky? Happy is a girl. Bernard is gay. Polly plays Charlie. We have ten directors and our entire set is doors. It might as well be *Hamlet*. It sure as hell isn't anything else."

Which I regret saying, because it may have been bad for morale. Anyway, I agreed to drop the idea, but, it was a great moment. I felt like an actress. Linda Loman came to life. And, something else happened. After rehearsal, guess what? Walt asked me for a date.

My name is Yvette Tuchinsky. I like realism in a name, but that's heroism. Now, my father, who paid for everything, wants me to keep it. But, how would that look: *Mame*: starring Yvette Tuchinsky? I can't live with that. So, what I decided to do was this: dump the name, keep the initials. Okay? I think that's a great compromise. Now, you try to find a name that begins with "Y." Because to me as an actress a name is very important. Oh, it's not major afterwards, but before, when you're trying to get people to notice you, the name can have primo value, and so I want a name that hits like a hammer on steel. Oh, I left out the most important thing. I'm in a play. A showcase of *Death of a Salesman* and I had to get my name by next week, so my picture in the lobby would be complete. Back to "Y." Yolande? Yetta? Yogie? I mean, what the hell begins with a "Y"? So, I invited Clark to come over and help me, but I did not ask him to bring that bottle of vodka. Yerdl? Yerdl Tucker? Yuppie? Yaphetta? Yabadaba-Trent? I was so frustrated. Then, how about just the initial "Y"? And my last name could be the letters of a powerful agency. And, I could be Y . . . MCA! Get it? And then, finally, it came. I loved it! Wow! I called and ordered a hundred prints. Are you ready? I hope you like it, because it's different. Yesterday Tomorrow! Well? That's my new name! No, I'm not kidding! Do you love it? It was inspired by Tuesday Weld. Yesterday Tomorrow? It sums me up. I'm the traditions of the past coupled with the excitement of the future. People can call me *Yes*! Do you like it? Be honest. We drank all the vodka. You hate it? You're not sure. Good. I told the producer and he loved it. He said:

"Well, now you can tell people that even though you weren't born Yesterday they can always call you Tomorrow."

Everyone else likes it. Anyway, it's too late to change and my father is coming opening night and I've already paid for a hundred prints. Jesus. I don't believe you. Yours is the first negative reaction. No. You're wrong. It's a great name. It just takes a little getting used to. Oh, God! I hate it! Maybe, I should tell my father not to come. A hundred prints! Oh, God. A hundred prints. Aagghhhhhh.

You won't believe this. We're doing *Death of a Salesman*. And who do I see on the street? On the corner of Broadway and 57th? Arthur Goddamn Miller! Yes! He wrote the play! He's tall, austere, almost bald, handsome. The man is handsome. And, Christ, with glasses, he looks so intelligent. I mean the man wears intellect by the yard. Of course, I'm sure. I know Arthur Miller when I see the guy. I'm standing ten feet away. He's by himself. I find myself following him. I want to catch up. I want to say,

"Arthur, I'm Ed Shray. And we're doing your play! Come and see it. You'll be comp-ed. You have to come. We love you. Arthur, we've taken a few liberties, but I know you'll love our ideas. Just keep an open mind. Arthur, the motif is doors. Seven doors and a refrigerator. Arthur, look at me. I worship you."

Which is my way of saying: I'm good, too, baby. I'm good, too. And he makes a left into this garage and in he goes. And he's gone. A tall stranger in a great sports jacket. A genius. MY genius! My playwright. Artie! This is no coincidence. Fate. I am so excited. I'm this close to being thrilled. Ed and Arthur. Pals. Oh, man. And I'm standing on the street; standing there in front of a parking garage in Manhattan, having clearly the biggest personal opportunity of my professional life and I can't leave. I must have one more look at him. A minute later, I get the chance. Here he comes behind the wheel of a black Mercedes. He passes me and makes a right onto 57th and then I go for it. I jump out into the street and start waving. This is my big chance. This is it.

"Goodbye, Arthur! Ed Shray. CIrcle 6-5491. Eight performances!"

He hears me. Arthur turns his head. He thinks he knows me. No! Oh! WHACK! He runs the Mercedes right into a parked Toyota. The crash of his headlight is the sound of my heart falling in pieces at my feet. Oh, my God. He's out of his car, facing me with bare hatred. He will never forget my face. All I can do is turn and run. I'm a running rat. I'm a producer fleeing down Broadway. Running away from Arthur Miller. Away from recognition and glory. Away. Now, could this be an omen? I don't think so. Because, was it my fault? Absolutely not. I was only trying to be awestruck. It's his fault! I am not taking responsibility and I am not going into some this-must-have-meaning panic. I'm a producer. I don't panic and I don't have meaning. I wave. That's all. And, it's not my fault if Miller can write a play, but still can't drive a fucking car.

No, this is too much. I can't take it. I'm playing the hooker in *Death of a Salesman* and Charlie, who plays Willy who buys me stockings up in Boston in Act Two, has started to blur the fine line between the play and today. First, he began to get way too familiar with his hands during rehearsal. Way too.

"Hey! Buster, you're acting! That's all. So, don't push it."

And I didn't even think that Charlie liked women. And he blushed and said he was sorry. Okay? Okay. So, naturally I went along with the first late-at-night phone call, because I think he must be kidding. Actors do that. So, then I go along with his second call, because perhaps he's improv-ing and he needs my help. Fine. I'm an actress. I'll help. But then came call number three.

"Hi, angel. It's Willy. I'm down in my room. Why don't you pop over? I've got six pairs of nylons. I'd love to see you try them on."

"Charlie, it's one in the morning. I have to get some sleep. Cut this out and leave me alone!"

He says, "Charlie? I'm Willy and I'm so lonely. You know how I get when I'm on the road."

"What road? You're in your apartment, you asshole! And don't send me any more flowers!"

"But, baby, this is your Willy."

"So, okay, Willy, take my advice and go home to your wife."

Which was probably the wrong thing to say. So, I hang up and the next day I complained to Ed our producer. And Ed says:

"But, his performance is growing. Think of it as an office romance"

"But Ed, I hate the office. That's why I became an actress! And this is called acting. Isn't it supposed to stop when we leave the theater? Or, is he in this for life?"

"But, we—"

"Call his answering machine! Call it! 'Hi, this is W. Loman. I'm not home. I'm in Boston.' He's in Boston alright. He's on the moon."

Ed was no help. So, I warned Charlie.

"Willy, you touch me like that again and this play will really be called *Death of a Salesman*. I'm going to knock your goddamned teeth out. Okay? . . . Willy?"

AND I HAVE TEN LOUSY LINES! . . . one more week and then eight performances . . . I never wanted this part. Never. WHY DO I HAVE TO BE THE HOOKER? IS IT MY ASS?

I have a rule. I try to never have sex with anyone in the cast during rehearsals. I mean during rehearsal weeks. Because it's wrong and it can mess up a performance. Love affairs and acting don't mix, but this *Death of a Salesman* time was so difficult that when Walt asked me out and took me home I was in a weakened condition and by one-thirty in the morning we were on the floor when who should come banging on my door? Yes! Willy Loman! How can this be? What on earth is he doing here? It's Charlie, barging in with sample cases and taking over the place . . .

"Hi, Linda. Hello, Bernard. How's the boy? Where's Biff?"

And before I know it, we're doing Act One. Act One in my apartment at one o'clock in the morning. A half hour later, Willy says:

"Well, I'd better be going. I have sales to make."

And just like that, the maniac is out the door. What nerve! I would say: "Who the hell does he think he is?" But, I already know. It's a nightmare. He's totally nuts. On the other hand, our scenes went very well. Caught off-guard, I just suddenly fell into being Linda, and I was very good. So good, in fact, that when Walt tried to resume our earlier mood, I was really offended.

"Bernard . . . really! Watch it! Or, I'll tell your mother."

I mean, he is the kid next door and, hey, I was just a married woman.

I was afraid this would happen, but I think I handled it well. Anyway, tension started to really build, and understandably, so when our lead playing Willy in *Death of a Salesman* got into a fist fight with our director. This never happened in college. It was awful. I almost cried. And now, even though I never really even did a full play in Montana, I'm not only directing a scene but I'm playing three small parts in New York. Oh, boy. And I've been living with Yvette, who is so wonderful, but these guys keep coming over: some actors, some directors, some even have jobs, and she asks me to spend hours in the bathroom. How many baths can I take? She says she doesn't go all the way, but may I ask, how many stops can you make until you arrive? So, last night, Ed, who hired me in the first place, asked me to come home with him after rehearsal to help him design a set. How could I say no? So, it was real late, and he suggested that I just crash on his sofa and all that, and then after a few minutes of lights out, sure enough, I knew it, he came padding over and said he was so keyed up, he just wanted to talk and massage me a little because he knew we were both tense and it would help us both to fall asleep and after a little bit of that, he said he could do a better job if he got all the way in with me because his back hurt, and eventually, I asked him if he loved me and I swear I could see him grow pale even in the dark. And he said,

"Well, Polly, I certainly like you very much."

But he didn't know if a man like him could ever love anyone, and then I told him about my promise to my boyfriend and he said,

"Oh, God, you, too! Damnit!"

and he excused himself and went off into the bathroom. I don't know for how long, because I fell asleep. In the morning, when I woke up, there he was back on the couch with me, but at the other end, sort of curled up, his head against my feet. I hope I didn't hurt his feelings, but this is one actress who will not sleep her way to the top. Anyway, curled up like that, Ed looked a lot younger than I realized. Younger. And really sweet; fast asleep against my feet. He didn't have any food in the house, not anything, not even juice, so we went out for breakfast.

Three days to go. I don't feel well. But, I must go on. I'm the associate producer. Ed gave me this honor when he got lost in his door fetish. So it fell to me. And I took it on not because I wanted to do, but because I had to. I'm directing certain scenes and I'm acting; playing Ben with an itch and a brogue. I don't know if the show is good. I don't know if the show is bad. I don't know what the hell the show is. Is it a show? All I know is that I have to oversee every goddamned thing except my performance. And I'm getting very nervous. Because I am doing too many things and I am getting very nervous. I put Polly in charge of the house and she's okay. We'll sell coffee at intermission and cookies. I lay out money for coffee. I don't like laying out money. I'm an actor, not a banker. Polly asks:

"What kind?"

I scream at her: "I don't give a shit what kind! COFFEE!"

She starts to cry. Good. An excuse to hold her. Oh, let me hold this girl. She is so soft, so sweet. I—

"Napkins? No. I'm not paying for napkins! If the audience wants to wipe their mouths, let them use their goddamned program."

I'm a good actor who is now also in charge of the bathroom. I'm so pleased. Maybe the critics can review the sinks. Perhaps, if I do well here, next year I can be scrubbing toilets on Broadway. And, I—wait! The lobby? Yes, I'm in charge. Why not? Lobby? A wino wouldn't vomit in there. And inside? Mine. A theatrical cathedral of forty seats and mushy carpeting that smells like lentil soup. And I have to act. I'm an actor. And the walls need paint and the little paint that's left needs a wall, and I'm an actor and our backstage has one sink, but no faucets, and I have to act. But, who needs faucets when there's no water? We bring our own! In soda bottles. I swear to God. And I have to act! Do you understand? In all of, beneath all, in spite of all of this misery, I must find a performance. And I will. I don't care if the lobby caves in or if the carpeting rears up and eats feet! I will give a great performance! Because, I—did I tell you that in college I was Oedipus? Oedipus The King! And now I'm Ben The Janitor. But, after this production, and that's what I must remember, there will be an after; I will go on. I'll recover and be stronger. Strong! Strong. Do you hear me? I'll be strong. But I will never work with Ed Shray again. NEVER! NEVER. Unless . . . it's a lead.

You want to hear about opening night? Okay. Listen. It was unbelievable. What a night. I was very good. Let me tell you what happened. As an actor, from an actor's point of view. All of a sudden, it all not only came together, it flew apart! But, not like a collapse, like a radiance, a spectrum of incredible performances. I have to give myself credit, because I have to. Who else is there to admit how good I was? Now, I'll be honest, I did a few things wrong, but the whole play, the entire *Death of a Salesman* took hold during my first big scene with Snappy when I'm talking about how much I'm inspired by mares and newborn colts. I swear, I didn't know that line was funny. But, what a laugh it got. So, then, for some reason, I started to giggle and then Snappy did her line about my being a poet and an idealist, and well the house came down, but not on our heads, on our side. And I laughed! And after that everyone was getting laughs. But, not cruel laughter; warm, loving laughter and I heard someone in the audience say:

"Funnier than Neil Simon."

In Act Two when it gets sad, because, come on, the play is a drama, the laughing stopped. Because we had become real people, by laughing with them, we had become no threat, no pretension, but real people. Striving, lost, dying people, all that crap. Hoping. Whatever people are. Sad? I mean it was good. Willy was wonderful. At the end, the applause was great, especially for Willy and you know Charlie deserved it. He was so goddamned good. I was proud. Can you believe that? I was proud to be on stage with another actor. He had come so far. Of course, I felt some jealousy. But, anyway, it wasn't even that he was very good, he was wonderful. He made that man live. Claire was fine, the girls were good, the only one who stunk was Jason. His foreign accent went from Scottish to Chinese. But, we'll fix that. Afterwards, we loved each other. We had performed in a wonderful play and moved people. I think that's why I act. Actually, I have no idea why. Who knows? But, tonight is our second performance. Why do we have to do it again? Who else in this world has to dig that deep night after night? Please, just let us be as good. Can we do it again? WE HAVE TO DO IT AGAIN! Hell, we can do it. We have no choice.

You know, if something isn't working, an actress just can't sit around. You have to take a chance. I'm playing Happy, a boy, as Snappy, a girl, in *Salesman*. Sleeping on the same door with my brother Biff is awkward enough, but all the dialogue we changed to suit me as a girl, just wasn't playing. So, after the first weekend, we said screw it. Let's put everything back the way it was, go for the original dialogue, and we did and the results have been outstanding. For instance; in Act One, my brother Biff talks to me about Big Betsy on Bushwick Avenue. The girl he fixed me up with, the first time I scored. And, then I thank him for teaching me all that I know about women . . . Well, you can hear the audience gasp. Pow! And the scene in Act Two when we're both trying to pick up women in a bar? Are we talking subtext, or are we talking subtext. What a difference. Now, some friends who saw the show said: "Yvette . . . what was that? What was that?"

But, I don't care. Because, I am Snappy, the world's first Loman lesbian. And it makes my character live. Y'know, the audience knows when you're taking a chance. They don't want us to fail, unless it's friends. No. The audience wants us to be all the things they aren't. I don't mean gay. I mean complete. Definable and brave. And as Happy cum Snappy: a lovely, pleasant, in-your-face, Flatbush dyke, I am suddenly all those things and more. There has been some booing. But I, Yesterday Tomorrow, (and my new name is really catchy) am acting as I have never acted before. Because when something isn't working, an actress must take a chance. You have to. Otherwise, buy a ticket and watch. But, tonight my dad is coming. So, naturally, I'm scared to death. Now, I'm going to change the subject and then I'll shut up. People come backstage so impressed, because to them being an actress is so difficult. No. It's not being an actress that's hard. Where do you go to get away? Where do you hide? And, oh, wouldn't it be just wonderful if Arthur Miller would write a script for all of us for the rest of our lives? . . . Wouldn't it be just grand? Thank you. And that's all I have to say. Over and out.

The final performance will go down in history. No. Maybe, up. We had a full house because we were a hit. And we gave them a *Death of a Salesman* that no one present will soon forget. And, I realize now that it had all been simmering; building up. It started backstage when Jason, playing Ben, and who had also done a first rate job with refreshments—he included wine—came up to me and whispered,

"I know where I've been in Africa . . . The Cameroons."

So, I said fine. Not knowing that when he came onstage he would do all his scenes in French. And, then, Claire playing my mother went totally incestuous on me; licking my fingers and ad-libbing some dialogue about us showering together. I bought it and actually just for a moment, fondled her jugs. The audience gasped, and then in my scene with my gay sister, I said good night by kissing Yvette on the mouth, what the hell, and she kissed me back and we fell on each other and went rolling to the floor. Nice. But that is nothing compared to what happened in Willy's Act Two flashback up in Boston with the hooker. And I know Anita's warned him, but this time when Willy patted her behind; no giggling. Anita decked him with a right cross that could have dropped an elephant! Willy was down. Down! Oh, it was great. But he got up and staggered back into the present; bleary-eyed and bloody! This was the play! This was Willy Loman. Down, down, Schmeling is down! YES! But, not out. Don't you see? OH! Willy Loman literally creamed and cross-eyed, but still game! Why? Why? Why, didn't I let her knock him out every night? What a finish. Lips oozing; knees buckling; five times Willy hit the deck. Five! He didn't know where he was. The audience was going wild; shouting:

"Get up, Willy! Get up!"

And he did, clinging desperately to some blind pride. At one point, I swear, he actually called me Linda and began doing dialogue from *Brigadoon*. Oh, this was theater, baby! This was the real stuff. *Death of a Salesman*? Not word for word, but who cared? It was theatrical excitement of a singular kind. By then, we were all lost. We didn't know where the hell we were. It didn't matter! Wherever we were, we were together! Go for it, actors! Screw the play! We ARE the play! Breathe a new life. Shock me with gesture. Shake me with your courage. And oh, the final scene at Willy's grave, with my weeping mother stroking my manly thighs, and Snappy, my gay sister, tongueing my ear, and Bernard there, (that was my idea, it's not in the script) with a purse, weeping hysterically for the man that got away. Well, you talk about dysfunctional? We had brought this forties-family into the nineties with a palpable roar of truth. Goddamn. We did theater! And, Willy wandered out. Yes! He thought the play was over. And, even Ben joined us, reeking of wine and humming the "Marseillaise"! Oh, baby! What a finish. Huge. The audience was on its feet. Bravo. Bravo. Okay, it was friends. But, they knew! A bunch of unknowns had done a play. Screw you, Arthur and your Mercedes. He would have loved it. I don't want to think about tomorrow. This is the night I want to savor. Savor. Delicious. Savor. Delicious. This is one I earned and never want to lose.

Oh, we had a great cast party. Ed, as producer, offered to pay for for everything. But, Ed, as actor, got so drunk he'd never remember saying that, and nobody believed him, anyway. We were at the back table at Gilleys, our hang-out, and we danced and sang and cried. A few friends came by. Most had been to the show and said that they had never seen anything like it. Does that mean that it was good? Claire was kissing Ed and Ed was kissing me. And then Charlie arrived from the hospital with Yvette, with wires in his jaw, because Anita had knocked him out in Act Two. And everybody cheered. He seemed lost. He wasn't Willy Loman anymore. There was a lot of compliments and everything got real misty. Even the waitresses got into it. Ed made a long incoherent speech that made no sense. Except, he said, as usual, none of the invited agents had made it down. Everyone booed. Jason threw up. I had to be at my restaurant by ten A.M. but, I didn't want to leave. Am I forgetting anything? I don't think so. And, other people had jobs, too, so about two we divided the check, left a pretty good tip and left.

"G'night. G'night. G'night. Love you. G'night."

That was three months ago and I now live with two other "real" waitresses. Walt phoned to tell me that Claire had gone to Buffalo and that Ed was acting in a tour of southern high schools in *Oedipus Rex*, so the group was probably not getting back together in the fall. But, he said, not to feel bad, most groups break up. Most groups break up. Oh, well. What the heck. Walt said an actor has to get used to that; to things breaking up. The show ends. Funny, but, when you're doing it, you never think it will. But, I'm buying the trades every week and something new is bound to turn up. And everybody left.

"Good night, g'night. I love you . . . Good night . . . ."

About the Author . . .

Ken Friedman was born and raised in New York City. Following four years in the Navy, he attended the University of Florida. He returned to New York and wrote material for Johnny Carson, The Bob Newhart Specials, the Dean Martin Roasts and others. His play *Claptrap* was presented by the Manhattan Theatre Club in 1987 and has had numerous productions in the United States and abroad. *60 For You* is his first book of monologues.